BAREFOOT

The Collected Poems

30127 08673818 9

MY FATHER, DYING

          succulent

1 At summer's mellow end,
   the house is green-stained.
   I reach for my father's hand

2 and study his ancient nails.
   Feeble-bodied, yet at intervals,
   a sweetness appears and prevails.

3 The heaviness of the night
   seems to get at his throat.
   It is as if the dark coughed.

4 Age has stained his face.
   In the other rooms of the house,
   the furniture stands mumchance.

       his
5 By the bed, the newspaper lies furled.
   He has suddenly grown too old
   to unfold the world,
         diminished

6 which has dwindled to the size of a sheet.
          opaqueness
   His room has a tenseness to it.
   I do not call it waiting, but I wait.
                  still

8 Confusing sleep and death,
   and anxiously to hover over
     the butterfly of his breath.
      which flits between sleep r death
      flitting

7 I shave him, feeling bone
   stretching the waxed skin
   cradling the wagged-out chin.
       his

9 There is so much to be said
   dear old man, before I find you dead.
   but we have become too separate

10 now in human time
   to unravel all the interim
   as your memory goes dumb.

          mostly
12 We have become no more than hands
   and voices in your understanding.
         hold
   The whole house is pending.

BAREFOOT

The Collected Poems

ALASTAIR REID

Edited
by
TOM POW

Galileo Publishers
16 Woodlands Road
Great Shelford
Cambridge CB22 5LW
UK

www.galileopublishing.co.uk

Galileo Publishers is an imprint of Galileo Multimedia Ltd

ISBN
978-1-903385-82-1 (hardback)
978-1-903385-81-4 (paperback)

First published in the UK 2018

Set in Adobe Caslon 13/15 by Iolaire Typography Ltd

Jacket design by NamdesignUK

Printed in the EU

I was the little barefoot boy,
the wind-willed pilgrim of your dreams.

Alastair Reid: from 'For You', *12 Poems*, (1 9 4 9)

Since I wore no shoes, Pablo and Matilde [Neruda] called
me then [1 9 6 4] and ever after, *Patapelá* (Barefoot).

From Alastair Reid's essay, 'Borges and Neruda' (1 9 9 6)

CONTENTS

ODDMENTS, INKLINGS, OMENS, MOMENTS (1959)

FROM PASSWORDS (1963)

FROM WEATHERING (1978)

* Previously unpublished or uncollected

AND FINALLY

ACKNOWLEDGEMENTS

One of the recurring motifs in Alastair Reid's writing is that of the instability of the self. He viewed himself rather as a constitution of 'selves'. The aim of this book has been to frame as clearly as possible the development of the self who was the poet. There have been anthologies that have presented a 'body of work' and he has himself provided the context in which much of it arose in autobiographical essays for *The New Yorker*.[1] But there has not been a book that has concerned itself with the 'work through time'. I hope that consideration of this trajectory, and of the choices he made, bring further attention to the pleasures and excitements of reading his poetry. This book is informed by many years of friendship, during which he shared aspects of his writing life with me. I have been helped by the archival research undertaken by his widow, Leslie Clark, in the National Library of Scotland. She has endeavoured to trace where the poems first appeared. Alastair Reid only very rarely dated his poems, so, apart from the broad chronology of the books themselves, often publication in magazines is the most accurate way of dating composition. I am honoured that Leslie and Alastair's son, Jasper Reid, have entrusted the work of editing *The Collected Poems* to me. My thanks are also due to Alastair Reid's long-time friend and agent, Thomas Colchie, and to my agent, Jenny Brown. I am grateful to the Pacheco estate for permission to

1   Many of these were reprinted in collections, on both sides of the Atlantic, such as *Whereabouts* (Edinburgh, Canongate, 1987) and *Outside In – Selected Prose* (Edinburgh, Polygon, 2008)

publish Alastair Reid's translation of 'High Treason' and to Susan Wood for permission to use her portrait of Alastair. Molly Perrin helped me, with professionalism and understanding, to prepare the manuscript. Robert Hyde at Galileo Publishers did the rest.

ABBREVIATIONS

As Alastair Reid was a friend of mine, it seemed unnatural to refer to him as Reid; but, in this context, not fitting to refer to him as Alastair. AR is how he frequently signed himself.

AR's papers are kept in the National Library of Scotland. Reference here will be to the NLS.

The title of the collection, *Oddments, Inklings, Omens, Moments,* once established, has been abbrieviated to *Oddments...*

Many of his poems and his essays, first appeared in *The New Yorker*. Any American spellings have been rendered into standard English for this publication.

INTRODUCTION

AR was born in Whithorn in South West Scotland in 1926. His father was a minister in the Church of Scotland, his mother a country doctor. From an early age, he realised that roots could be dislodged; one of his earliest fantasies was to follow the tinkers and travellers who came to his parents' door. After war service in the Navy (1943-46) and a degree in classics at St. Andrews University, he moved in 1949 to the United States. Although translation and the essay became dominant forms in his writing life, it was as a poet that he began. In the 1950s, he started to publish poems in *The New Yorker* and to develop a relationship with the Spanish world that would last the rest of his life. For many years, *The New Yorker* was his only reliable postal address. In 'Hauntings', one of his essays, he describes how a friend had to paste extra pages into his address book to accommodate 'more than forty permanent addresses for [him] since 1950, dotted all over Europe, Latin America, the United States'.

In 1949, AR published *12 Poems*. It was privately printed in St. Andrews in an edition of fifty signed copies. The author was twenty three and they are the works of a poet finding his voice through other voices. The undertones of Yeats and Auden are clear:

> Be still, and I will gather my words slowly,
> weighing each one for its worth with a craftsman's care.
>
> ('Be Still')

These are not AR's first published poems; five poems appeared in *Scottish Student Verse 1937-1947* with an introduction by Eric Linklater,[2] one of which, 'Underworld', appears in his first full volume, part of a sequence about the sea. It would not have fitted this suite of *12 Poems* about the bitter-sweet end of love affairs, where emotion and the poet's words are mocked by the 'troubled touch of time'. There is some costume-wearing here, but there are also fragments that suggest awareness of an individual process:

> I did not make my poems from thought,
> or hope, or metaphysical decisions
> but out of the web of my days, from dreams half-caught
> and frail lost visions.
>
> ('IF YOU SHOULD READ MY POEMS')

12 Poems is drawn from a series of over fifty poems, the majority unpublished, which bear the cover sheet, 'Poems' at the top and at the bottom, 'Alastair Reid, St. Mary's Manse, SELKIRK'.[3] Many of the poems touch on his war experiences: 'When I joined the Royal Navy, in the later years of the war, I was projected abruptly out of Scotland and to sea, on a series of small ships, around the Indian Ocean – endless ports of call that were all astonishments.'[4] Several of the poems draw directly on place – 'To Arab Boatmen, Heard Singing on the River', 'Dhows Passing', 'For An Indian Lady' – but the most successful poems concern a more reflective response to his experiences. These press against the tight forms he chooses, as in the sonnet, 'Travellers' Tales', whose ending echoes '*Dulce Et Decorum Est*':

---

2   In his introduction to *Scottish Student Verse*, Linklater had written, 'The newest poets in the Scottish universities have not shrugged off their experience of war, but keep it to live with; and a consequence of their bitter association is that these pages offer more than 'university verses'. They sometimes offer poetry.'

3   AR's father, William Arnold Reid, accepted a larger charge in Selkirk in 1931, when AR was starting school. He left it in 1948, when AR was 22.

4   From 'Hauntings' (*Whereabouts – Notes on Being a Foreigner* – Edinburgh, Canongate, 1987)

Child, do not listen. I will tell you stories
of these far off lands, and dim your dreaming joys,
of cities built of dust, poor painted glories,
children who dream as you, but have for toys
hunger and pain and blood, tears and death.

Elsewhere, there are feelings of entrapment. In 'Hauntings', AR writes: ' …forgetting made the war much easier to survive than remembering. It scarcely arises now, either in memory or in dream, for I have instinctively enclosed it in a warp outside real time. It makes no more sense in the memory than it did in its nightmare reality.' This may account for the absence of even the best of these, often elegiac, poems from AR's published work.[5] Yet they remain valuable documents, as historical evidence of how a gifted young man uses poetry to make sense of complex experiences and, in the poetic development of AR, demonstrations that, this early in his career, he is able to refine experience and to extract from it essential truths.

One of the *12 Poems*, 'Autobiography', reappears in his first full collection, *To Lighten My House*. 'Autobiography' carries within it two of AR's enduring subjects – the passage of time and a love of song. Song or poetry, representing the apprehension of experience in language, is seen throughout AR's work as an (attempted) intervention in the flow of time:

Now autumn haunts me with the fear of losing
anticipation, and the power of song.

This collection was published in 1953, a mere four years after *12 Poems*. The poet was now twenty seven and there are twenty

---

5   Apart from those poems in the 'Selkirk Manse' folio, there is no evidence that AR will write poems again - even indirectly - about the war.

seven poems in the collection. AR had crossed the Atlantic and the book was published in New York where he was living.[6] There had been a remarkable unbuckling and growing in such a short space of time.[7] But then, he was hardly young in terms of experience. As a nineteen year old cipher clerk in the South Moluccan Straits, in August 1945, he had decoded the message, 'Cease all offensive operations against the Japanese. Cease all offensive operations against the Japanese.'

Seldon Rodman, a prolific man of letters, commented on the fly cover of AR's first American publication that the poems, 'give promise that their author will be that long-awaited figure, the heir to Auden and Dylan Thomas.' One poem, 'Isle of Arran', certainly bears the imprint of Dylan Thomas' heightened sense of remembrance:[8]

> Where no one was was where my world was stilled
> into hills that hung behind the lasting water.

However, a comparison with a companion poem, 'Maine Coast' is instructive. In it, and even more so in 'New Hampshire', we can see the apprehension of the moment, a more focused attentiveness to the world. At times, one is reminded, in the sharp imagery of the latter poem, of the work of his fellow Scot, Norman MacCaig - both shared 'a Scots accent of the mind':

> Deer have been known to tiptoe down for apples.
> A snake may suddenly scribble out of sight.
> Your eyes are never sure. Each evening,
> someone comes back from almost seeing a bear.
>
> ('NEW HAMPSHIRE')

---

6   AR was teaching at Sarah Lawrence, a Liberal Arts College, fifteen miles north of Manhattan, after an initial spell teaching in Iowa.

7   Extracts from letters sent to his friend John Main at the end of the Notes capture the excitement and the creative energy that AR felt at this time

8   Dylan Thomas died in New York in the same year *To Lighten My House* was published.

Coupled with this freshness, there is a keen perception - one that will weave through his work and make him such a sympathetic translator of Borges - regarding the permeability of the self: 'we must listen to the wise/ wind saying all our other selves are lies.' ('Maine Coast')

Unsurprising that the 'foreigner' – the name he eventually gave to frame his (self-willed) experience of displacement – would be an aficionado of maps. 'Directions for a Map' is an extended meditation on journeying through space and time (and between cultures) in which the attention to detail of Elizabeth Bishop is coupled with the mythic nostalgia of Edwin Muir:

> …looking backwards,
> we missed the comfort of the old illusions,
> the tall, alleviating gods, the travellers;
> and, mindful of those fruitful days,
> we often wished for angels in the wind -

The poem is the most powerful example in this volume of a poet's growing confidence in his own creative possibilities – and in literary worlds on which he can now draw. The volume also contains several reminders of AR's delight in play,[9] finding form in songs, spells and nursery rhymes – Walter de la Mare was, after all, an early interest – but the most significant change of tone in this volume, from *12 Poems*, is the casting off of Romanticism's borrowed coat. In its place, there is a stronger sense of the authority of lived experience, of what he had shown in the early, unpublished 'war' poems – as in this description of 'The Village':

> No one moves here but children and ancient women,
> and bees haunting the edges. The village hangs
> with more intensity than a heavy dream.

---

9 AR's love of 'playfulness – 27 poems for 27 years – was one of the reasons he made such a fine writer of books for children.

Oddments, Inklings, Omens, Moments followed in 1959. AR was now 33 and of the 33 poems in this collection, thirteen have appeared in *The New Yorker*. The title poem ends, 'love occurs/ like song, like weather',[10] three of his recurring themes emphasising imaginative continuities in a life of increasing geographical change. Like Robert Graves, with whom AR spent time in Mallorca and whose poem-portrait is included here, and like Borges, AR knew copious amounts of poetry by heart. In his early work, these models can appear to be insufficiently processed, but in *Oddments* ... influences are at the companionable service of his own voice. In 'A Lesson for Beautiful Women', one of a number of love poems, there is the shadow of Andrew Marvell amplifying the resonances of the poem; while in 'In Such a Poise is Love', behind the closing lines—

> Who has not, in love's fever,
> insisted on one simple vow, 'for ever',
> and felt, before the words are gone,
> the doom of them dawn?

— lies the sonorous, but clear voice of Graves himself. An interesting comparison at this time might be made with Thom Gunn. Three years younger than AR, Gunn moved to California in 1954. His poetry there became stylistically bifurcated; his options included the formal, classical metres he brought with him and the influences he adopted there – the open forms of Ginsberg, Snyder and Duncan. AR wrote with the same companions as Gunn – Marvell and Donne – but he worked within the familiar traditions of Frost, Bishop, Lowell and Wilbur.[11] In fact, in his reserve, his Latin American 'self' and the scrupulous curating of his own work, Bishop may be his closest American spirit.

---

10   In the essay, 'Notes on Being a Foreigner', AR writes, 'The beginning of poetry for me was the dazzling realisation of all that seemed to be magically compressed into the word "weather".'

11   It would be Edwin Morgan who would introduce the American practitioners of 'voice'/breath into Scottish poetry.

Elsewhere, in *Oddments ...*, AR adapts songs and fairy tales to his own purposes. In many of these, he favours short lines, a skipping rhythm. Poems, like 'Once in Piertarvit', convey the conviction of the imagination at play. One thinks of Mercutio's Queen Mab: 'True, I talk of dreams,/ which are the children of an idle brain', or, as AR expressed it all these years before, 'dreams half-caught/ and frail lost visions'.

One of the most powerful of the dreams in this book is 'The Tale The Hermit Told', a dramatic monologue about a magically lost village. The poem is set in Spain. However, not in form, but in feeling, the poem recalls the Scottish uncanny as expressed in ballads like 'Thomas the Rhymer' and narrative poems, like 'Tam O'Shanter'.

> I was standing, nowhere, horrified, alone,
> waiting for her eyes to appear and laugh
> the afternoon back...

Weather and mirrors, two of AR's recurring motifs, represent for him the instability of the self. In 'Cat Faith', he writes, 'Slowly the room arrives and dawns, and we/ arrive in our selves ...' But which self? 'To see I am the same,/ I speak, in my own voice.' ('Spain, Morning') Nothing is taken for granted in a collection in which the question becomes a stylistic strategy:

> Do the dead lie down then? Are blind men blind?
> Does love rest in the senses? Do lights go out?
> And what is that shifting, shifting in the mind?
> The wind?   ('GHOSTS')

There is, at last, a questioning of the capabilities of language itself:

> The point is seeing – the grace
> beyond recognition, the ways
> of the bird rising, unnamed, unknown,

beyond the range of language, beyond its noun.
Eyes open on growing, flying, happening
and go on opening. Manifold, the world
dawns on unrecognising, realising eyes.
Amazement is the thing.
Not love, but the astonishment of loving.

('GROWING, FLYING, HAPPENING')

Four years later, in 1963, AR published *Passwords – Places, Poems, Preoccupations*. It contains fifteen new poems embedded in a series of essays, travel pieces written for *The New Yorker*, and shorter conceits about language and the alphabet. On its back cover, AR writes, 'Poems are for me the consequences of the odd epiphanies which from time to time miraculously happen; prose I keep for a calmer, more reflective everyday attention to the world.'[12]

Passwords is framed by two significant essays – 'Notes on Being a Foreigner' and 'The Transformations: Notes on Childhood'. The book is an exploration of the restless state of the 'foreigner', rather than a definition, and the poems are part of this process, drawing added resonance from their context. A brief bestiary of owls, cats and frogs help to advance the argument. 'Curiosity' makes the foreigner's existential choices our own:

> A cat minority of one
> is all that can be counted on
> to tell the truth. And what he has to tell
> on each return from hell
> is this: that dying is what the living do,
> that dying is what the loving do,
> and that dead dogs are those who do not know
> that dying is what, to live, each has to do.

---

12 In his essay on Graves, he writes, 'For him, poems were not just sudden pieces of writing: they were events.' This would make both Graves and AR members of what Douglas Dunn has called, 'The miraculous school of writing.'

The instability of self that the foreigner risks is echoed in the fragility of relationships, beset by psychological and geographical distance:

> Now that the sea begins to dull with winter,
> and I so far, and you so far,
> (and home further than either),
> write me a long letter
> as if from home.
>
> ('ME TO YOU')

In 'Notes on Being a Foreigner', AR writes that 'what haunts the foreigner is the thought of always having to move on, of finding, in the places where he comes to rest, the ghosts he thought were left behind; or of losing the sharp edge, the wry, surprised eye that keeps him extra-conscious of things.' The eye is rooted in the 'limitless present' of childhood that, on occasion, graces the adult:

> ...every now and again, one of these moments occurs, so transcendent in its immediacy, so amazing in its extraor-dinariness, that we get a sudden glimpse of what child-hood was all about and how much the present has receded before a cluttered past and an anxious future. In these odd moments, the true memory of childhood dawns.
>
> ('TRANSFORMATIONS...')

Edwin Muir held to the belief that life is experienced through two lenses: The Story (a life's individual trajectory) and The Fable (its shared, mythic dimension). For Muir, the forced departure from his Orcadian childhood was his own expulsion from Eden. AR never shared Muir's belief system, but certainly his relationship with the loss and rediscovery of his own childhood landscape in Galloway carried similar import. However, as ' ...the family ghosts fade in the hanging air', and 'Mirrors reflect the silence,' AR must acknowledge:

Marooned in cities, dreaming of greenness,
or dazed by journeys, dreading to arrive -
change, change is where I live.

'The Spiral', from which these lines are taken, closes *Passwords*.
At thirty seven, the poet has identified his situation and found a
language – honed by practice, experience and thought – to express
it. In 'Notes to Being a Foreigner', he has also acknowledged that
' …to be a foreigner is not, after all, a question of domicile, but
of temperament.'

It was another fifteen years before AR published *Weathering*, a
selection of poems and translations. Of the sixty four poems,
twenty eight are new ones.[13] The poems are organised themati-
cally, allowing poems to complement or to spark off each other.
This would be his principle also in *Inside Out*, a selected poems
and translations published in 2008.[14] Writing of his own *Collected
Poems 1965-2016*, Frank Bidart comments, 'The aim throughout
has been not chronology, but a kind of topography of the life we
share …'[15] AR's topography is clear to readers of his work, but the
aim of a collected is to deepen appreciation of continuities and
development. There are, for example, themes in the new poems
that amplify or affirm those AR has been exploring for some
time. One of these is the interplay between place and self. In a
number of these encounters, he comes to similar conclusions.
Returning to New York, he discovers that 'Only my name is the
same' ('New York Surprised'), while, in 'Geneva':

In this town of telling, we grow old
in a tumble of bells, and over us alleviating

---

13   A twenty-ninth, 'Mediterranean', had been published as 'Casa d'Amunt' in *Oddments* … There were
     minimal changes to it under its new title – a reminder perhaps that Graves too was a renowned
     fiddler with previous versions of his work.

14   *Inside Out – Selected Poems and Translations* (Edinburgh, Polygon, 2008)

15   *Half-Light*, New York, Farrar, Straus and Giroux, 2017

in the continuum
time falls, snow falls, words fall.

In 'Daedalus', he sees change as part of our natural imaginative world, envisaging his son's selves as birds – 'wren, hawk,/ swallow or owl'. He questions:

Am I to call him down, to give him
a grounding, teach him gravity?
Gently, gently.
Time tells us what we weigh, and soon enough
his feet will reach the ground.
Age, like a cage, will enclose him.

Not for the first time in his poetry, there is an echo of Dylan Thomas's ending to 'Fern Hill': 'Time held me green and dying/ Though I sang in my chains like the sea.'

In his questioning of appearances and of the unreliability of language, as someone more and more preoccupied with translation – a ghost who lives 'in a limbo between two worlds' ('What Gets Lost/ *Lo Que Se Pierde*') – AR finds he has an affinity with Borges: 'I have kept coming across my own preoccupations, and writing English poems out of what is concealed in the Spanish.'[16] Nevertheless, in several poems here, the restrained musicality in the control of rhythm, assonance and rhyme makes personal poems, like 'My Father, Dying' and 'Weathering', among his finest achievements, for he manages to imbue them with the 'spoken intimacy' he so admired in Neruda's work.[17]

'Scotland' is skewered here in his most widely anthologised poem, but the 'punchline' of the old woman's response about the beautiful day: "We'll pay for it, we'll pay for it, we'll pay for it."

---

16   From a letter to Anthony Kerrigan, Barcelona, Summer 1963.
17   AR met Neruda in February 1964 at his house in Isla Negra. Since he went barefoot, Neruda and his wife, Matilde, called him ever after, 'el poeta patapelá'. It was at that time that Neruda first asked AR to translate a sheaf of his poems.

only resounds because of the skill with which AR sets it up; the physical delight in the moment:

> The grasses
> shivered with presences, sunlight
> stayed like a halo on hair, heather and hills.

AR's argument with Scotland was never with its landscape.

There is no evidence of diminution of AR's skills or in the spirit with which he ended *To Lighten My House*: 'I wake in/ the nowhere of the moment, single-willed/ to love the world.' And yet, famously, the collection opens with a preface by AR (a first) in which he comments, 'I look on this book as something of a farewell on my part to formal poetry, which seems to me now something of an artificial gesture, like wearing a tie.'[18] It is a sentiment that can perhaps be discerned in the 'weather' of 'The Academy', his reflection on a return to visit his *alma mater*, St. Andrews University:

> I do not think much of the academy
> in the drift of days. It does not change. I do.
> This poem will occupy the library
> but I will not. I have not done with doing.
> I did not know the truth there, nor did you.

And if AR was 'done' with poetry, he was certainly not 'done with doing'. *Weathering* already lists six books by Neruda and five by Borges he had either translated or edited and, in the 'calmer, more reflective everyday attention to the world' of his essays, he is producing what Andrew O'Hagan describes as, 'among the best prose writing to have emerged from Scotland over the last hundred years'.[19]

> For possibility,
> I choose to leave behind

---

18 Something he hated. 'Disguises' ends: 'I sit in my stubborn skin and count/ all clothing is disguise.'
19 From his introduction to *Outside In, Selected Prose*.

each language, each country.
Will this place be an end
or will there be one other,
truer, rarer?

('THE SPIRAL')

AR's concerns with identity and with language – his own desig-
nation of 'foreigner' – make his work pertinent to experiences of
dislocation in our time. His movements were not forced on him,
but his perception of how culture and place shape reality – and,
in his poetry, 'reality' is always questioned – make him a poet of
continued relevance. Moreover, in his restless states – a poet with
footholds in (and influences from) Scotland, America and the
Spanish world – change passed through him. In spirit, Scotland
moved towards AR, not the other way round. He experienced
the shadow of Franco and saw Spain re-integrated into Europe.
Along with John Berger, he has much to say about (the demise
of) village life.[20] He saw Latin American poetry lauded, the poets
forerunners to 'el Boom'. Of course, he was too subtle a poet to
deal with (much of) this material directly, but it does have a
shaping awareness in his poetry. He had a reputation as a nomad,
but his poems are not travelogues; rather they are ontological
probings of what living in unfamiliar contexts tells *us* about our
existence. Perhaps he felt he had explored these circumstances
through the lyric poem as far as he wished. He wanted to go
deeper, more capaciously, into place. And deeper into language.
Perhaps, in exploring the many branch lines of translation, he
felt he was exploring new selves. As Mireille Gansel put it,
'Translation is also about taking the byways that lead to distant
places. The ultimate refuge: poetry as the language of survival,
of unassailable liberty.'[21] Translation, the choice of tinkers and

---

20 With Berger, he appreciated that 'to emigrate is always to dismantle the centre of the world, and so
to move into a lost, disorientated one of fragments' (from Berger's *And Our Faces, My Heart, Brief as
Photos*); although, as a 'foreigner', he would make no such claims for himself.
21 From *Translation as Transhumance* by Mireille Gansel (London, Les Fugitives, 2017).

travellers, suited him. 'A good translator,' he recalled Graves had told him, 'must have *nerve*.'

AR loved islands, as this collection attests, and I would urge readers to regard each poem as an island to settle on for a while, with the proviso that 'Home/ is where new words are still to come.' ('Visiting Lecturer'). There are poems here that I am confident will 'occupy the library', but there is one to consider at the end. 'Weathering' is the poem we all wish to grow into. Throughout AR's work, weather is portrayed in a negative way – the instability of emotion, unwanted or unpredictable change. Here, in its active sense, there is a beneficence about it:

> Weathering. Patina, gloss and whorl.
> The trunk of an almond tree, gnarled but still fruitful.
> Weathering is what I would like to do well.

In the poem, 'Two Weathers' (in *Oddments* ...), AR asks, 'Why should they run so counter,/ outer and inner weather?' 'Weathering' suggests he has found (temporally or not) a balance between his many selves and the natural world, or, to put it another way, 'equilibrium, home'. ('Galilea')

CALL BACK THE DAYS
(EARLY POEMS)

1943-49 (?)

CALL UP

I saw the footworn track,
and knew that now there was no turning back,
no time to pause, or wait
for lingering backward glances from the gate.
The rippling meadow-grass
hissed out a hushed farewell on seeing me pass,
and round my venturing feet,
the sunspots danced. The pinewood scent was sweet.
Oh, it was hard to leave
a happiness that time might not retrieve,
hard, too, to leave you there,
your brown eyes sad, and summer in your hair.

THE NEW WAY

There was not much trouble in that goodbye
—in the saying of it, I mean. But the way
was that untrodden one, that lay
over the thick of the older wood,
and not very often had I gone there,
but mostly by one where the grass was bare
and footpath clearer, with sometimes the eye
of a cottage lamp to point the way.
But this was a night I wanted away
to a different place, in my different mood.

So I left the road for the higher places
and found the wood—but the path was strange,
having no known tree-trunks to mark its range.
It was dark, for the boughs shut out the sky
where they bent close over. And owls would call
to the world that the snow was beginning to fall
Oh my steps were slow there. Ways, like faces,
grow dear with knowing, and going through
is easy. But this was strange and, I knew,
was bound to be dark where I'd said goodbye.

LEGACY

No, I will give you only shadowy things,
and everything in tides, with a tang of the sea,
broken glass for your toys, or feather free
gull-skeletons sunk in the sand, sea-shiverings,
snatches of sleepy song, a laughter-gust,
and weird wind-wrinkled sailors' eyes, and cries
strange from the swirl, and drownings, and goodbyes,
bare feet blue with the cold, eyes red with rust,
and stinging tears from the windy whine, and a bare
shelter scratched in the sand, wet nets that flap
forlornly, tales from the tides that, lonely, lap
your shadow, winds that wither your words to air,
laughter for your love—oh hide your head
in dreams, forget what the sea, once sorrowing, said.

Hospital Afternoon

This deepening quiet comes with the afternoon,
and some men, lying back, forget to gaze
at that one spot their eyes have fixed all day,
and close their wondering minds, and sink to sleep.
Others gaze restlessly about the ward.
Their minds move with their eyes. They wonder where
to turn to now from their white-sheeted prison.
Somewhere a wireless plays itself to sleep
behind the scratching of the nurse's pen.
Some old tune, tiptoeing on the atmosphere,
calls and then dies. But men, lying there, will hear,
will feel this fresh wind through their dusty dreams
and cast their thoughts on it, and feel them blown
through the new opened windows of the memory.

Travellers' Tales

O child, I watched your gentle eager eyes,
bright with the firelight and the gold spun story
of that old traveller's word-woven glory,
and watched the colours of a far sunrise
glow in your little soul, and new dreams brighten
in the gay opening palace of your heart.
When tales are told and travellers depart,
the fires go out. But dreamed-of dawns still lighten
this air of fantasy, your child-sweet breath.
Child, do not listen. I will tell you stories
of these far lands, and dim your dreaming joys,
of cities built of dust, poor painted glories,
children who dream as you, but have for toys
hunger and pain and blood, and tears and death.

Call Back The Days

Call back the days, the heedless happy days,
the winter-white delight, the summer joy,
the light forgotten laughter of the boy,
the gathering world, the new discovered ways,
the waking mind, the first strange stir of knowing.
Turn back awhile to pages lit with laughter,
turn through the chaptered years, and coming after,
feel the first touch of time, the growth in going.
    Remember—then the wondering sad years
come suddenly with their sound of falling days
where wandering has blurred familiar ways.
Come out of time awhile to the sunsweet places
where there are no sad shadows, no time-tears,
only the songs, the dear remembered faces.

Torchlight Procession

Along the way the torchlit column goes
wildly. And watching, I remember those
who marched along with me to the last sad turning.
They bore no torches, but their hearts were burning.

[Scottish Student Verse 1937–47, 12 Poems]

Tomb

One hollow sun-bleached bone, and a ragged feather
the wind had ripped from the wing of a rotting gull,
and separate prints in the sand beginning to dull
were all we left on the tomb of our time together.

We two will mourn, perhaps, that the best is over
in parting—but never so much as the wind will moan
of its greater grief in the hollow haunted bone,
torn feather, and footprints it breathes on the sand to cover.

[*Scottish Student Verse, 1937–47, 12 Poems*]

AND WHEN THE SUN ...

And when the sun sends longer shadow fingers
to point the hour for peace, the men move home
to rest, weary from labour. No one lingers
to watch the gold surrender to the shadow
and evening stillness settle on the meadow.
And none will watch, from sleeping windowsills,
how the great clouds move grey over the loam
to stretch their sky-worn lengths along the hills.

[*Scottish Student Verse, 1937–47, 12 Poems*]

NOCTURNE

I take no comfort from the dark,
mistrust the shadows' sympathy,
fearing they do a black night's work
for death, the dawnless enemy.

Above my head tonight I feel
the trees' relentless scimitars,
the moon a grinning yellow skull
among the crossbones of the stars.

[*Scottish Student Verse, 1937–47, 12 Poems*]

TO LIGHTEN MY HOUSE

1953

I

Poem Without Ends

One cannot take the beginning out of the air
saying "It is the time: the hour is here".
The process is continuous as wind,
the bird observed, not rising, but in flight,
unrealized, in motion in the mind.

The end of everything is similar, never
actually happening, but always over.
The agony, the bent head, only tell
that already in the heart the innocent evening
is thick with all the ferment of farewell.

Poem For My Father

When my father first made me in a Scottish summer
he heard various voices. There was trouble in the islands;
but the act of love was an evening matter, a heart-beat
that ran wild in the blood and swelled and burst and was silence.

So born, I was blessed. The impatient heart-beat hurrying
hard over heather-grown hills, the green wanton sea
splintering wild in the cave and becoming the quiet
wash of the ultimate wave, translating itself into me.

And I think of the quiet way my father had
with his hands which were for blessing, which blessed a tree
unconsciously with their touch. And how it was spring on the island
when he reached out and first felt birth: leaves and life: the same mystery.

But then it was different, difficult, with dark weathers engraving
the unlucky island, imposing their winter's worth
of lack: and across the firth the black procession
of blown clouds flying from their unfulfilling north

and sickness running the sullen length of Scotland:
rocks, roots encrusting with years, all the field fallow,
the land unfurrowed, dryness invading our living,
the weight of a war, waste, and worse to follow.

Away now, it becomes a bit of the bone, carving
a cross of a kind, a root in the restless land

when the waves lap over the world and the voices quiver.
Away, the island is a secret held, with hope, in the hand.

But the mind must find its own way back to the bone
and the beginning. Only the blood's blind intellect
tells, when it talks, a truth like stone, corrects
the present, and later leads back to all that this life lacked;

but only begins. Bare rock. And the rest is not only growing,
but building. The inarticulate island offers its choice
of suffering. I choose to achieve the spring, work against winter.
So choosing, I take my vows and become its voice.

And out of the times that tear at the roots, at love,
I begin, with root and with love, to build. And remembering birth,
the act of my father's love, and his faith, I reach
with his hands to bless again the bare potential earth.

Lay For New Lovers

In the crux of the dark O under a lemon moon
    lying below the lap of the barn
being lovers we were born   being warm and lovers
and sick with a secret O and the ogling owls
fell sideways out of the thinning dark
and our limbs were liquid and longed to tell
    under the lap of the barn
    in the cup of the dark

In the drip of the day in the early damp of the dawn
    in beads on the brow on the wood of the barn
love over we were worn   being cold and over
and hollow with having loved and the morning birds
were crossing the windows of the early light
and our limbs were lazy and limp with knowing
    under a melon sun
    on the lip of the dawn

In the red of the dawn in the day of an awkward age
    under the cloud of an unconcern
unloving we lie alone   being left and lonely
and lured from a love in the blood now when the hawks
are sweeping a morning out of the simple sky
and we love in a moment left out of the world
    under a slipping sky
    in the sleep of the day

MY ONE HIGH MORNING

My one high morning is the green beginning;
but who could speak across the singing time
of trees and finger-tips where halfwinds worry
a love so easy on the wordless hillside
my anxious sentences all try to climb?

You hold the morning in your hands, its meaning
mostly a song in the blood. I become a tree,
limbs all longing, leaves all eager, loving.
The sap spills out of my root and spells a secret
in sudden green spontaneous certainty.

Currents cross in the lake. Tremendous silence
is all I hold: old words are worn away.
I want to touch and tell your truthful body
this first transforming secret, and awaking
I want to give you all my life away.

BOYHOOD

The day he first began to be boy
was a different shape, was strange. His world was trouble
and trees were shaped like girls as the day grew human
    and gave him
a handful of painful photographs
to go to bed with in the stinging dark.

The night door closed but never on sleep
while he groped with nightmares in his dogeared pillow
telling his puzzling day under a patchwork cover
to find the easy thread that ravelled
his restless boyhood on a sheet of night.

But every door would burst with morning
wide on a boyish sun and set his feet
chasing a shout across the clear and arrogant fields
under a sky all young and shy with secrets
saved to be solved in the puzzled pillowed dark.

To Look In The Heart

It becomes more difficult to look in the heart.
Time brings the easy answer to the tongue.
The eyes learn all the different disguises.
Hands play a simple superficial part.
Even the foot is scarcely once put wrong
and for lover or lawyer, days hold no surprises.

Passion and patience, all are finger-tipped
held at the end of an eyelash, well-defined.
Only the automatic words are said.
Behind the masks, the skeleton waits, thin-lipped,
while all the clockwork attitudes unwind
and the wasted heart, without a voice, goes dead.

GRANDFATHER

Age was detachment. Out of world and time,
both dead in his bad body, he saved a wind
    with the last of his green love,
ruffled his white-haired years with wizened fingers,
made windy tales from the spells of his sailing life.

Age was release. Past anxious mountains of future
he unbent his graybeard back in an easy strath.
    His words had waterfall strength
when this last blue interval left him a boy's breathing,
and a deep down laughter allowed a joke at death.

Age had no motive. Free of desire and act,
he founded summertimes and doubled dreams
    in between genesis and grief,
and with cleanheaded children close to their first ocean,
lived out in his end the lost boyhood of angels.

THE VILLAGE

This village, like a child's deliberate vision,
shimmers in sunshine. Cottages bloom like flowers
and blink across the gardens thick with silence.
No one moves here but children and ancient women,
and bees haunting the hedges. The village hangs
with more intensity than a heavy dream.

But turn, and you will find the mountains watching
almost in judgement, like stone sentinels
over your shoulder, critical as eyes
behind the screen of distance, keeping watch.
Nor in midsummer ever be deceived
by silence, or by villages at peace.
Behind your house, those hollow hills are hearing
your quietest thoughts, as loud as thunder.

[*The New Yorker, August 23rd, 1952*]

AUTOBIOGRAPHY

A boy, I was content to cling to silence.
The first years found me unprepared for spring.
April spoke quickly with a quick excitement.
My sudden voice was too surprised to sing.

Year followed year, the faithful falling seasons.
My voice was never confident for long.
Now autumn haunts me with the fear of losing
anticipation, and the power of song.

[*Scottish Student Verse 1937–47, 12 Poems*]

NOT NOW FOR MY SINS' SAKE

Not now for my sins' sake,
nor for Adam or anyone
a memory might wake,
do I take this breaking day to grieve,
not for today's Eve
perpetually weeping in the nibbled apples,
and not for all the lost or too alone.

Not grief for the old-headed children, running
wild in their redletter days,
nor for my longlegged and living girl
dancing to meet me down her fabled ways—
these dear selves shelter in the now of love.

No. Past praise for the world, young once at least,
I come always to grief at last,
not for my death
or the presently splintering world,
but for all failing love
gone waste in words and reasons
down the noiseless tick of the breath,
down all our warring life.
Always again writing my lettered grief,
I hold my changing self, for this instant stilled,
and hold this crisscross world,
love crossed with loss, the cycle of all the sad seasons.

The Day The Weather Broke

Last out in the raining weather, a girl and I
drip in the hazy light while cars slur by,
    and the single drizzling reason
    of rain in an alien season
turns us to each other till a train arrives,
to share, by bond of wetness, our wet lives.

Although, for talk, we can find to put our thumb on
    only the rain in common,
is this what love is—that we draw together
    in the inhuman weather,
strangers, who pool our sheltered selves and take,
    for the sky's sake,
this luck, to be caught without our usual cloak
    the day the weather broke?

Song For Four Seasons

Held and spelled in a golden fold,
I wished to find a windfall in the orchard—
    held in a summer wind,
I found beyond the well the cidered boys
tempting their sweethearts in the trampled apples.

Going down a dropping autumn sky
I feared to find a spider in the apple—
    going down a falling field,
I found behind the well a longlegged maiden
loving her boy among the stubbled barley.

Stilled and cold in a frozen field,
I hoped to find an apple in the graveyard—
    stilled in a winter waste,
I found beside the drying well a woman
watching the spiders spinning out a shroud.

Climbing a green and growing day,
I grieved to find a grave among the barley—
    climbing a springing hill,
I found above the brimming well a baby
blowing time to pieces on a dandelion.

II

SPELL FOR FIVE FINGERS

The winds and planets beautifully spinning
called for letters and numbers, whirling
   over the counted world.

I found a world in my hand.
A five-starred fist of senses
   finger-tipped the time.

I found a world in the winds.
The elements were seasons
   in the quarters of the heart.

I found a world in my wishes.
Head, heart and hand, three guesses.
   My luck went three times round.

I found a world in the mirror.
The day and night were doubles.
   My eyes were black and white.

I found a world in my head.
The sun was one within me.
   My shoulders wore the globe.

One was a word, was a world, was wonder.
Zodiacs, alphabets, calendars tumbled.
The moon made mock of the almanack.
　The maps remembered the weather.
The scale was a spell, the spell was a measure,
the measure was music, the harmony, love—
　and I held the world in a word.
The wonderful numbers spun in a measure.
The letters like lovers were wound in a spell.
The light of the breath was calling the changes

　—and over and over the heart beat time.

The Question In The Cobweb

The frog beneath the juniper
warns us where the terrors are,
crouched below a creaking root
grunts of water underfoot.

Draped on a branch above, the crow
croaks a crude judicial No,
forbidding with a beady eye
any wayward wish to fly.

Furtive flowers in flower beds
hear the wind and bend their heads.
A shiver by the river warns
watch for cows with crooked horns.

A rumble in a tumbled cloud
is mumbling of rain aloud.
A hedgehog humping home alone
makes thunder underneath a stone.

The spider with the knitting legs
purls a puzzle round his eggs.
A nimble stilted centipede
worries a secret in a seed.

Waving leaves like windmill sails,
the tallest elms are telling tales.
A rumour in the garrulous grass
plays havoc with the weatherglass.

Somewhere clocks begin to chime,
telling what we think is time;
meanwhile, the sundial on the lawn
is baffled by the falling sun.

The meadow with the mayflower hair
breathes a last question on the air,
while overhead the homing bees
buzz with private mysteries.

And like some last inquisitor,
the frog beneath the juniper,
crouching in a question mark,
croaks his password to the dark.

[*The Atlantic, December 1952*]

Music Box

Pricked out on pins of time, a tune from nowhere
whirrs on a hairspring hidden in the ears,
and, listening through a microscope, one hears
a spiderweb of sound plucked out of air.

A little twig-legged dancer in a trance
on wooden tiptoe, wearing a whiff of wool,
pirouettes wildly as a ticking spool
unwinds the inches of her watchspring dance.

Watching, a plump and pumpkin-coloured clown,
perched on a miniature wirework music stand,
counts careful waltztime with his pinhead hand,
the baton slowing as the box runs down.

Too small for minds. The image suddenly shatters
as somewhere, clumsily, a great clock clatters.

SATURDAY PARK

With a whiff of a Saturday summer, the park
attracts its people in lazy rows.
The pigeons perform and the squirrels eat bark
but most of them gaze at each other's clothes;

and the green goes back and the birds are leaving
and nothing is said, for a stopped hour's sake.
In the midst of the lost there are some of them living—

the little red girl on her roller skate wheels
giving the turning world a try,
and the hobnailed boy showing arrogant heels—
young enough to know why.

Designs For Three Dancers

I

Her wish explodes in legs,
and through all the hullaballoo hoops of her jumping joy
      come bounding with a growl
the sudden burly goblins of her dream—

  wishes to whirlwinds, a witch to a woman,
  cartwheel capers on a cobwebbed common,
      out of a rafter after a wind,
      streaming a rumour of hair behind
        to loosen the whims
        in the windmill limbs
        as all our alarms
        come alive as arms,
  and the child in the terrible skin uncovers
  the trace in the trees of the tiptoeing lovers
  who leave in the leaping air, like an angel,
      the strange little girl
      on her wing-footed stage
        (stranger than age)
  while a harp plays havoc and a cello-voiced cow
  remembers and moos to the yellow-eyed daisies
      the ways of an endless loving world
  to the wandered girl in the wishbone curled—

this is the way the muscles sing her name.

II

Once upon America there was a time,
cried the little red hobnailed boy we called Dogear,
    and fell down laughing

and his crazy storybook with its foxed pages
blew into atoms of laughter on a tellpie wind
    and that was the end.

    He was a poet, that boy.

III

No, none of the meadows remember now how her feet
would space them on tiptoe in these mornings of light
down the unprinted grass, princess of air,
fleet-footed, cat-footed, carrying a secret,
light as a falling feather, all alone.
        Through all these days alone
she walked with the weathers turning in her head.

Unwinding a new dance now, in wisps from her feet
she discovers again the spell of her playground days,
the telltale ways of her body, queen of now,
wise as a cat, and wayward to her lover,
old with the fallen world, no more alone.
        So, turning over her life,
she spins through this bright night with a star in her head.

NURSERY SONGS

WHO CAN SAY

Mother, I went to China this morning.
The trees were pagodas, the puddles were seas.
Dragons were hiding behind the begonias.
      I was a mandarin.
      Willows were bowing.
      Lies, lies, said she.
      And I hid from her frightening eyes.
        who can say, who can say?

Children, the gardens belong now to goblins.
The willows spread legends, the waterfall plays.
Fairytales wind like a web round the window.
      Goodnight to all birds now.
      The night's wings are folding.
      Lies, lies, said I.
      But I hid from her wonderful eyes.
        who can say, who can say?

Three Sides Of A Penny

Heads, said the one and the penny spun,
bright as a bullet in the delicate sun.
 choose choose
 win or lose
Who tells true to the tossing copper?
Nobody guessed at a gust of wind
and the coin came down in the sea.

Tails, said the other and the penny turned over,
hovering in air like a wavering lover.
 tell tell
 head or tail
Who calls true to the tumbling copper?
No one allowed for a gambling man
and the penny dropped in his hand.

Said the gambling fellow, either will do.
Anyway who split the penny in two?
 one not two
 both are true
I call yes to the coin in the sky.
One two three and the world goes round—
and he threw the penny away.

NEW HAMPSHIRE

Here, green has grown to be a habit.
The hills are forest-headed, not for farmers.
Trees hug the land as close as fur.
A lake looks naked. There is no way in,

except for local animals. And the roads
stumble and lurch down humps of stubbled dust.
Flowers bloom at ease without being told
and grass has grown untidily, in a hurry.

Here, the tall elm and the leaking maple,
and apple trees as gnarled as farmers' knuckles
ooze stickily with sap or syrup.
Forests are tumbled to make room for trees.

Houses are hewn and hidden in the hedges,
all pine and wooden pegs. The paths are lost.
Towns are a pilgrimage away.
Here, families live alone in hand-made homes.

Only the animals are seasoned owners.
The lakes belong to frogs with broken voices.
Farms are inhabited by rabbits.
A fox barks like a landlord down the dark.

Deer have been known to tiptoe down for apples.
A snake may suddenly scribble out of sight.
Your eyes are never sure. Each evening,
someone comes back from almost seeing a bear.

Here, space is sweet with extra air. The silence
is positive, and has a steady sound.
You seem to own the woods, until
a shotgun coughs, to warn you, in the valley.

A week is a whole anthology of weather.
The country has you somehow at its mercy.
The size of the moon begins to matter,
and every night, a whippoorwill leaves omens.

All names are hung on stilted mailboxes,
spasmodically fed with last week's letters.
The children quickly learn to wave.
A summer changes strangers into neighbours.

Here, one is grateful to the tolerant landscape,
and glad to be known by men with leather faces
who welcome anything but questions.
Words, like the water, must be used with care.

III

Four Figures For The Sea

I

Inside the crook of the blackened beckoning headland
five winters since, the sea drew down this drifter.
The drowned hull found the sand.

Five winters' water and the tides' long fingers
undressed like nibbling fish its driftwood ribwork.
    Barnacles cobbled the keel.

Overboard now, in weeded prisms of water
the crusted woodwork hulk wavers, forever
    safe in the fossiling sea.

Stilled like the little galleons old men's fingers
bottled and sealed, it lies, a sand-shelved skeleton
    stayed in the glass-topped bay.

So in the glass of words, I stay the sea.

II

We only remembered the sea in his faraway eyes.
But under a sailing moon, on cots of foam,
the sea brought back his sodden, foundered body.
   The long waves rolled him home.

All the long night, he drowned in our waterlogged nightmares.
The swollen tide drained out of his flooded heartbeat.
Nightlong, he lay beside the subsiding water
   and the sea ran out of his eyes.

III

Here is the shell, the sea made flesh, and spinning
through threaded webs and whorls
flowered in your giant fingers,
your history is this graph
of graven hieroglyphics.
These intricate pink nets
hold change and chart your life.
Tracing the lacy spiral,
enmeshed, the eye turns inward.
The heart of the shell is shadow.
Inside, you cannot see.
But listen, ear to the sea's ear,
and hear, rising and falling,
the pulse at the turning centre—
your heartbeat and the sea.

IV

Over the walking foreshore cluttered
black with the tide's untidy wrack,
and pools that brimmed with the moon,
I trespassed underwater.
My feet stained seabed sand.
The night wore guilt like a watermark;
and down the guilty dark,
the gulls muttered to windward.
Far out, the tide spoke back.

Across the morning clean of my walking
ghost and the driftwood litter,
singly I walked into singing light.
The rocks walked light on the water;
and clouds as clean as spinnakers
puffed in the sea-blue sky.
A starfish signed the sand. Beyond
I faced the innocent sea.

Underworld

Sailors will tumble an old boat head over heel
for a turtle-turned house, and crazily cut a door
in its planks. They take the underside deck for a floor
and poke two pottering chimney pipes through the keel
for their driftwood fires. They have hammock beds, and
     a hatch,
and sea-gear—but never they know, as they lie unsleeping,
their hull-home is haunted by waterless old wood, weeping
when the clock goes wild, ringing bells at the turn of
     the watch.

  Because of the crime of changing a ship-shaped thing
so suddenly into a lurching hunchbacked shelter,
I'd be afraid, so afraid of the sea at evening,
afraid of the portholes, to find fish goggling there,
and a green strange undersea light beginning to filter
in through some drowned man's seaweed-swirling hair.

[*Scottish Student Verse 1937–47, 12 Poems*]

The Seasons Of The Sea

The cycle of the water rolling landwards
is shaped in the sailor's tale of a mother sea
and the eyes of men remembering their islands
from the harbour-masted wharves of a huddled town
   on a windy coast where the beating tides
break into births and deaths on beginning beaches
with mourning gulls to tell the nine waves' labour

To a boy by the tarry wood of the knotted pierstakes
lost in the windward look of a sailor dream
when the hymns from the churchlit windows danced on the water
she would come with the thud of men going down to the dawn
   their rubber boots stubbing the grubby decks
of the boats that nibbled their ropes with a rusty ringbolt
waiting with whining wire at the water's end

And later as lad unloading the groaning hold
he would taste the salt that crisped on hands as her knife
slit into the slithering breasts and her limber fingers
danced in the nimble nets for a whistling price
   blowing a kiss to the luck of the catch
as she counted the tumbling fish that gasped to death
in the round and bountiful basins and boxes of salt

Under the lingering looks from the buzzing pierhead
when she walked there the bay would wrinkle with voices
from the rocking boats that she loved with her eyes
in the playing water by the knocking spar
    with blown hair sprayed on the wind as her word
silenced the swarthy men in their black desiring
when she laughed with her teeth the length of a limb away

Until the nights in the netted loft when as maiden
she would sink in the swimming moon and make a prayer
of the tides of her heart to take her breathing lover
the boy with secrets to find in her skylight bed
    wound in a net of moonlit limbs
all the loose winds would lie with her kissing mouth
to drown his boyhood in her fumbled hair

A seawife's curse on children born in a storm
by draughty lamps in the doom of a harbour home
with her motherhood wet on her hardened hands she suffered
her luckless urchin on a turning tide
    on the ebb of a love that spilt and spent
its warmth on the twisted mouths of barren women
changing the joy of the loins to a waterfront shame

After to dread her name in the shipyard whisper
of lips by the lamps to lure the emptying men
with oaths on their mouths and dirty sailor money
for easy love below a drunken noon
    friendly legs in a brassbound bed
and her morning strut beneath the leering mastheads
buying the eyes of the lads with a crimson tune

At the last to grow in the lying lovers' moon
to the sight of a fishless sea and the sense of a grief
that sank in the net as she took the touch of ages
and lay alone in the pool of a cycle life
  and all the moons and crossing tides
talked in a graveyard sleep to tell her children
the tidy words above her driftwood stone

And fishbones white in the silt of a seaweed harbour
will take the tale to its end on a drying bay
to begin again in the ooze of a tide returning
to crabs in the pools and pockets of the rock
  linking the chain of the baffled love
that anchors the endless man to his sailor living
alone in a loft with the fish falling back in the sea

The Waterglass

A church tower crowned the town,
double in air and water,
and over anchored houses
the round bells rolled at noon.
Bubbles rolled to the surface.
The drowning bells swirled down.

A sun burned in the bay.
A lighthouse towered downward,
moored in the mirroring fathoms.
The seaweed swayed its tree.
A boat below me floated
upside down on the sky.

An underwater wind
ruffled the red-roofed shallows,
where wading stilt-legged children
stood in the clouded sand,
and down from the knee-deep harbour
a ladder led to the drowned.

Gulls fell out of the day.
The thrown net met its image
in the window of the water.
A ripple slurred the sky.
My hand swam up to meet me,
and I met myself in the sea.

Mirrored, I saw my death
in the underworld in the water,
and saw my drowned face sway in
the glass day underneath—
till I spoke to my speaking likeness,
and the moment broke with my breath.

[*The New Yorker, November 22nd, 1952*]

DIRECTIONS FOR A MAP

I

Birds' eyes see almost this, a tidy island
dropped like a footprint on a painted sea.
But maps set margins. Here, the land is measured,
changed to a flat, explicit world of names.

Crossing the threads of roads to tattered coastlines,
the rivers run in veins that crack the surface.
Mountains are dark like hair, and here and there
lakes gape like moth holes with the sea showing through.

Between the seaports tiptoe dotted shiplines
crossing designs of latitude and language.
The towns are wearing names. The sea is titled.
A compass stamps the corner like a seal.

Distance is spelt in alphabets and numbers.
Arrows occur at intervals of inches.
There are no signs for love or trouble, only
dots for a village and a cross for churches.

Here space is free for once from time and weather.
The sea has paused. To plot is possible.
Given detachment and a careful angle,
all destinations are predictable.

And given, too, the confidence of distance,
strangers may take a hundred mural journeys.
For once the paths are permanent, the colours
outlast the seasons and the death of friends.

And even though, on any printed landscape,
directions never tell you where to go,
maps are an evening comfort to the traveller:
a pencil line will quickly take him home.

II

Afraid at first,
they hid from that enormous, nameless sky.

Beyond their well-known neighbourly horizons,
anyone was a stranger, dangerous,
possibly armed, and never to be trusted.
Only the sailors brought back stories, roaring
news of the drunken east. What was the sea?
Water, they hoped. But not true blue.
Deceitful as a drug, a chronic liar.
Their gods were often angry. Notwithstanding,
a globe was growing strangely in their heads.
    A few had dreamed and listened.
Ptolemy, telling the sun on the blank sand,
was not afraid to say *incognitus*
        and keep his head.
Meanwhile, the earth was anybody's guess.
Mercator, straightening a later landscape,
crisscrossing Europe with meridians,
was hardly happy. Trouble and his errors
gathered like cobwebs in his attic rooms.
Only old Blaeu, below his golden sundial,

made peace with all the angels.
What was a map? His brush moved through blue water
and soothed the vellum sea. His eyes were azure.
Letters paced out his oceans. Thumbnail galleons
stayed everlastingly in sight of land.
The unknown poles were playgrounds laid for dolphins.
Alone, his wonder easily unwound
a starred and palette-coloured world
on charts as haunted as a mermaid's dream.

   But still the unfathomed, many-monstered sea
took toll, and tightened sailors' mouths.
Now there were charts to blame. Over their names,
the waves wore numbers, therefore errors.
Fear faltered still too often on the tiller,
till the instruments took over—
astrolabes stabbing at the sky for figures,
safe from all human failing and from hearsay,
the trade routes flagged with information,
the poles stuck thick with banners, and
the compass turning permanently home.
The figured winds withdrew, and Atlas rested,
the globe no longer heavy on his hands.
Down went Atlantis, mourned by dreamers,
greener among the skulls and mouldered bones.
The crest of Everest alone resisted.
Where was there left to go? We held the world.
    Light years away, in space,
some star was winking like an eager girl.

Light years away, but here, we stared
across the abyss between the map and us,
and wondered what was missing. In the nights,
nightmares knocked often in our heads, our days
were just as difficult. The end, we found,

was not a map, but here, and a beginning.
So we had guessed.
      But looking backwards,
we missed the comfort of the old illusions,
the tall alleviating gods, the travellers;
and, mindful of those faithful days,
we often wished for angels in the wind—
come back, old Boreas, even you are welcome;
Zephyrus merry in the west, young Auster,
sunbearing Eurus, we remember you.

III

Look through the map at now. This present island
wakes and takes on an unpredictable day.
Thin mists are nuzzling the uncanny mountains.
A boat is trying its luck on the knitted bay.

Birds blow about. Northwards, a wind is rising.
By the wall, the woollen sheep are keeping warm.
The sun makes patchwork on the oatmeal meadow.
The clouds take up positions for a storm.

Here we have never been. These moors are strangers.
The road we guessed is lost beyond the hill.
Miles have no meaning now. The gulls are frightened.
There are no arrows other than the will.

Names will not help. The signpost chokes with ivy.
Lightning winks. The sky is coming down.
The map is pocked with rain, and clapping thunder
calls time to ships across the rain-crossed town.

Somewhere behind a blurring village window,
a traveller waits. The storm walks in his room.

Under his hand, a lamplit map is lying.
Pencils tonight will never take him home.

IV

    Across the plot of the land
falls the long shadow of the pilgrim hand.
    A wind in miniature, the breath
troubles that country as withdrawn as death.
Though, safe from weather and the ways of love,
    these maps will never move,
the moving eyes, the island in the mind
    have their own maps to find.

    So grant to us again
    the courage to begin,
    to wish the morning well,
    to kiss before we tell,
    to trust enough to choose,
    to take our days as news.

    Here, in this trackless time,
    where habit is our crime,
    the amazing day begins,
    forgiving us our sins,
    and as we turn to bless,
    the landscape answers Yes.

V

A globe-eyed child finds first a map for wonder.
Her sea is scribbled full of ship-shaped fish.
Playing with all the names like spells, she tells
the time in Spain, and sails her fingers south.
Europe is torn: the world has no dimensions.

America is half the size of Rome.
Also, since here is now, all maps are nowhere.
This is a wishing world, where towns are home.

She marks a cross for luck, and lastly colours
a puff-cheeked cherub in the bottom corner—
      which terrifies a folded fly
who, tired from crawling foodless over Europe,
was crouching in the margin, contemplating
the little cipher of the maker's name.

Maine Coast

These islands are all anchored deep dark down.
Pines pitch-thick, gnarled green, and rich of root,
logs lying, lopped boughs, branches, broken rock,
the bow of a boat, the length of a life, weed-water.
I am an island, this is nearest home.

Time is called morning, clinging moist, mist-ridden.
Days are disguised, the houses are half trees—
wind in the attic, sea in the cellar, words
all alien. Though sun burns books, blinds eyes,
I see through to the bone and the beginning.

Tomorrow waits for the net; today tells
time in circles on the trunks, in tides.
Boats are lucky, love is lucky, children
are kings—and we must listen to the wise
wind saying all our other lives are lies.

[*The New Yorker, June 28th, 1952*]

Isle Of Arran

Where no one was was where my world was stilled
into hills that hung behind the lasting water,
a quiet quilt of heather where bees slept,
and a single slow bird in circles winding
round the axis of my head.

Any wind being only my breath, the weather
stopped, and a woollen cloud smothered the sun.
Rust and a mist hung over the clock of the day.
A mountain dreamed in the light of the dark
and marsh mallows were yellow for ever.

Still as a fish in the secret loch alone
I was held in the water where my feet found ground
and the air where my head ended,
all thought a prisoner of the still sense—
till a butterfly drunkenly began the world.

[*The New Yorker, 12th July, 1952*]

To Lighten My House

Somehow come to the calm of this present, a Sunday in summer,
here, held and steady under the spread sky,
   I set this christened poem loose
     to lighten my house.

Rising, my eyes and the sea, for ever and this time more,
meet; and across the anonymous sea-shaped bay,
   the wind, my life, and the ground beneath
     all turn on this breath.

Far away, over several lives and this sea, Scotland is ageing,
the shape of a humped sea-horse, mountain-headed,
   holding that kind and harboured home
     where I found my name,

on the inherited, mapped island I loved by its first name,
Arran, hunchbacked and hazy with family secrets,
   where, quartered in tidy seasons, I woke
     into shelters of talk.

My father's grave voice preaching, in a parish rich with fishermen,
the chanted parables for faith, while a dark god
   stormed in the unworded nights and wild eyes
     of the boy I was,

the hard-bitten heather on hills, the drowned bird nursed like a sister
wearing death in its sweet breast, all spelled my fear
   on the frightened nightfalling sea where I sailed,
     growing up and growing old—

years where my head, turned loose in burning chapels of doubt,
turned back on my blood, with all the words for journeys—
   war, and a war in my body to break
     that one way back.

I tell my stilled years to the sea, but the sea moves and is patient,
bearing all bottled wishes, faithful to all its fables,
   promising islands that will ask me back
     to take my luck.

Yet not in these seafared years, borne now in all my choices,
but in this firstborn day, in my opened house,
   are my hands handed the chance to love
     down one dear life.

And patiently into my bruised dark house, light breaks like a birthday
as, shouldering the weather of this place, I wake in
   the nowhere of the moment, single-willed
     to love the world.

ODDMENTS, INKLINGS, OMENS, MOMENTS

1959

WAS, IS, WILL BE

It was to have been
an enchanted spring—
the house friendly,
the neighbours kindly,
the mornings misted,
the birds soft-breasted,
the children easy,
the days lazy
with early flowers,
the time, ours.

Not as it is—
days ill-at-ease,
a plague of crows,
the first leaves slow,
the children jumpy,
the cook skimpy,
slant rain in streams,
goblin dreams,
the roof leaky,
work unlikely.

Or will be later
when, like an old letter,
the past stiffens
and afterthought softens.
Yet distant in winter,
I still will wonder—
was it we who engendered
the spring's condition,
or a ghost we had angered
with expectation?

[*The New Yorker, March 30th, 1957*]

A Game Of Glass

I do not believe this room
with its cat and its chandelier,
its chessboard-tiled floor,
and its shutters that open out
on an angel playing a fountain,
and the striped light slivering in
to a room that looks the same
in the mirror over my shoulder,
with a second glass-eyed cat.

My book does not look real.
The room and the mirror seem
to be playing a waiting game.
The cat has made its move,
the fountain has one to play,
and the thousand eyes of the angel
in the chandelier above
gleam beadily, and say
the next move is up to me.

How can I trust my luck?
Whatever way I look,
I cannot tell which is the door,
and I do not know who is who—
the thin man in the mirror,
or the watery one in the fountain.
The cat is eyeing my book.
What am I meant to do?
Which side is the mirror on?

[*The New Yorker, April 23rd 1955*]

GHOSTS

Never to see ghosts? Then to be
haunted by what is, only, to believe that glass
is for looking through, that rooms too can be empty,
the past past, deeds done,
that sleep, however troubled, is your own.
Do the dead lie down then? Are blind men blind?
Does love rest in the senses? Do lights go out?
And what is that shifting, shifting in the mind?
The wind?

No, they are there. Let your ear be gentle.
At dawn or owl-cry, over doorway and lintel,
theirs are the voices moving night towards morning,
the garden's grief, the river's warning.
Their curious presence in a kiss,
the past quivering in what is,
our words odd-sounding, not our own—
how can we think we sleep alone?

What do they have to tell? If we can hear them,
their voices are denials of all dying,
faint, like a lost bell-tone, lying
beyond sound or belief, in the oblique
reach of the sense through layers of recognition ...
Ghost by my desk, speak, speak.

[*The New Yorker, April 5th, 1958*]

ONCE AT PIERTARVIT

Once at Piertarvit,
one day in April,
the edge of spring,
with the air a-ripple,
and sea like knitting,
as Avril and Ann
and Ian and I
walked in the wind
along the headland,
Ian threw an apple
high over Piertarvit.

Not a great throw,
you would say, if you saw it,
but good for Ian.
His body tautened,
his arm let go
like a flesh-and-bone bow,
and the hard brown apple
left over from autumn
flew up and up,
crossing our gaze,
from the cliff at Piertarvit.

Then, all at once, horror
glanced off our eyes,
Ann's, mine, Avril's.

As the apple curved
in the stippled sky,
at the top of its arc,
it suddenly struck
the shape of a bird—
a gull that had glided
down from nowhere
above Piertarvit.

We imagined the thud
and the thin ribs breaking,
blood, and the bird
hurtling downward.
No such thing.
The broad wings wavered
a moment only,
then air sustained them.
The gull glided on
while the apple fell
in the sea at Piertarvit.

Nobody laughed.
Nobody whistled.
In that one moment,
our world had faltered.
The four of us stood
stock-still with horror,
till, breaking the spell,
Ian walked away
with a whirl in his head.
The whole sky curdled
over Piertarvit.

I followed slowly,
with Ann and Avril

trailing behind.
We had lost our lightness.
Even today,
old as we are,
we would find it hard
to say, without wonder,
"Ian hit a bird
with an apple, in April,
once at Piertarvit."

The Rain In Spain

Unmediterranean
today, the punctual sun
sulks and stays in

and heavily down the mountain
across olive and pine
rolls a scrim of rain.

Faces press to windows.
Strangers moon and booze.
Innkeepers doze.

Slow lopsided clocks
tick away weeks.
Rudely the weather knocks

and starts up old ills,
insect-itch, boils.
The mail brings bills.

Lovers in their houses
quarrel and make promises
or, restless, dream of cities.

Ghosts in the rafters mutter.
Goats thump and clatter.
Birds augur water.

The Dutch poet is sick.
The postman kicks his dog.
Death overtakes a pig.

Books turn sodden-sour.
Thunder grumbles somewhere.
Sleepers groan in nightmare,

each sure that the sky teems
with his personal phantoms,
each doomed to his own bad dreams.

For who is weather-wise
enough to recognise
which ills are the day's, which his?

[*The New Yorker, June 28th, 1958*]

Poet With Sea Horse
for Robert Graves

Though not apparently, you choose it well,
the hippocamp, with its twirled tail,
its odd body, its well-known nose,
its reputation for staying always upright
in spite of wild waters and turgid seas.

Once, it could enchant the boy you were.
Now, however, your enchantment has grown older,
has weathered the ravages of love, has stood
its share of moons and tides. Yet, erect still,
you keep the same features and enquiring head.

Such things stay with us, the bone
shaped oddly, the laugh unerringly our own,
our earliest enchantments. So may you always
ride out, like it, the curling tides, and stay
as rare, as solemn, and as resolutely gay.

CAT-FAITH

As a cat, caught by the door opening,
on the perilous top shelf, red-jawed and raspberry-clawed,
lets itself fall floorward without looking,
sure by cat-instinct it will find the ground
where innocence is; and falls
anyhow, in a furball, so fast that the eye
misses the twist and trust
that come from having fallen before,
and only notices cat silking away,
crime inconceivable in so meek a walk,

so do we let ourselves fall morningward
through shelves of dream. When, libertine at dark,
we let the visions in, and the black window
grotesques us back, our world unbalances.
Many-faced monsters of our own devising
jostle at the verge of sleep, as the room
loses its edges and grows hazed and haunted
by words murmured or by woes remembered,
till, sleep-dissolved, we fall, the known world leaves us,
and room and dream and self and safety melt
into a final madness, where any landscape
may easily curdle, and the dead cry out ...

but ultimately, it ebbs. Voices recede.
The pale square of the window glows and stays.
Slowly the room arrives and dawns, and we
arrive in our selves. Last night, last week, the past
leak back, awake. As light solidifies,
dream dims. Outside, the washed hush of the garden
waits patiently, and, newcomers from death,
how gratefully we draw its breath!
Yet, to endure that unknown night by night,
must we not be sure, with cat-insight,
we can afford its terrors, and that full day
will find us at the desk, sane, unafraid—
cheeks shaven, letters written, bills paid?

[*Poetry, February 1st, 1959*]

WHO AM I?

Could it have been mine,
that face—cold, alien—
that an unexpected mirror,
crossed by a quick look,
flashed me back?

It was a moment's chance,
since, at second glance,
the face had turned familiar—
my mouth again, my eyes
wide in surprise.

Now, though I verify
oddness of bone and eye,
we are no longer one,
myself and mirror-man. Trust has gone.

I had thought them sure,
the face and self I wore.
Yet, with no glass about,
what selves, whose unsuspected
faces stare out?

[*Poetry, February 1st, 1959*]

An Instance

Perhaps the accident of a bird
crossing the green window, a simultaneous phrase
of far singing, and a steeplejack
poised on the church spire, changing the gold clock,
set the moment alight. At any rate, a word
in that instant of realising catches fire,
ignites another, and soon, the page is ablaze
with a wildfire of writing. The clock chimes in the square.

All afternoon, in a scrawl of time,
the mood still smoulders. Rhyme remembers rhyme,
and words summon the moment when amazement
ran through the senses like a flame.
Later, the song forgotten, the sudden bird
flown who-knows-where, the incendiary word
long since crossed out, the steeplejack gone home,
their moment burns again, restored
to its spontaneity. The poem stays.

GROWING, FLYING, HAPPENING

Say the soft bird's name, but do not be surprised
to see it fall
headlong, struck skyless, into its pigeonhole—
columba palumbus and you have it dead,
wedged, neat, unwinged in your head.

That that black-backed tatter-winged thing
straking the harbour water and then plummeting
down, to come up, sleek head a-cock,
a minted herring shining in its beak,
is a guillemot, is neither here nor there
in the amazement of its rising,
wings slicing the stiff salt air.

That of that spindling spear-leaved plant,
wearing the palest purple umbel,
many-headed, blue-tinted, stilt-stalked
at the stream-edge, one should say briefly
angelica, is not enough (though grant
the name itself to be beautiful).
Grant too that any name
makes its own music: that *bryony, sally-my-handsome,*
burst at their sound into flower,
and that *falcon* and *phalarope* fly off in the ear,
still,
names are for saying at home.

The point is seeing—the grace
beyond recognition, the ways
of the bird rising, unnamed, unknown,
beyond the range of language, beyond its noun.
Eyes open on growing, flying, happening,
and go on opening. Manifold, the world
dawns on unrecognising, realising eyes.
Amazement is the thing.
Not love, but the astonishment of loving.

[*The New Yorker, May 2nd, 1958*]

At First Sight

Should I speak unthinkingly,
rashly, outwardly,
or look, wordlessly?

Move determinedly
or wait expectantly?
She sighs slightly.

I turn anxiously.
She sits quietly,
smiling distantly.

Either lie, passionately,
or not lie, fruitlessly?
I pause, two-mindedly.

To love wishfully,
blindly, entirely,
self-transformingly;

or to stay truthfully
in doubt, wistfully
doomed to reality?

Her face, held beautifully,
looks at me questioningly.
I watch her, wonderingly.

To love recklessly,
hazarding certainty,
losing identity;

or to feel warily—
vows made conditionally,
words weighed carefully?

She looks up suddenly,
her eyes speaking clearly
my thought, completely.

Poised unbelievably,
we touch magically,
and light strikes, blindingly.

Calenture

He never lives to tell,
but other men bring back the tale

of how, after days of gazing at the sea
unfolding itself incessantly and greenly—
hillsides of water, crested with clouds of foam—
he, heavy with a fading dream of home,
clambers aloft one morning, and, looking down,
cries out at seeing a different green,
farms, woods, grasslands, an extending plain,
hazy meadows, a long tree-fledged horizon,
swallows flashing in the halcyon sun,
his ship riding deep in rippled grain,
the road well-known to him, the house, the garden,
figures at the gate; and, lost in his passion,
he suddenly climbs down and begins to run.
Dazed by his joy, the others watch him drown.

Such calenture, they say,
is not unknown in lovers long at sea

yet such a like fever did she make in me
this green-leaved summer morning, that I,
seeing her confirm a wish made lovingly,
felt gate, trees, grass, birds, garden glimmer over,

a ripple cross her face, the sky quiver,
the cropped lawn sway in waves, the house founder,
the light break into flecks, the path shimmer,
till, finding her eyes clear and true at the centre,
I walked toward her on the flowering water.

[*The New Yorker, July 19th, 1958*]

In Such A Poise Is Love

Why should a hint of winter
darken the window, while the insects enter,
or a feel of snowfall, taking corners off
the rough wall and the roof,
while the sun hanging in the sky
hotly denies its contrary?

As if it knew all future will entail
probable tempered by improbable,
so the mind wanders to the unforeseen,
and the eye, waking, poises between
shock and recognition—the clothes, the chair,
bewildering, familiar.

In such a poise is love. But who
can keep the balance true,
can stay in the day's surprise, moving
between twin fears, of losing and of having?
Who has not, in love's fever,
insisted on one simple vow, 'for ever,'
and felt, before the words are gone,
the doom in them dawn?

FOR RING-GIVERS

Given the gift of a ring,
what circle does it close?
What does it say, passing
from lover to lover?
That love, encircled so,
rings for ever?

Or is it the round of love?Does the ring say
"So must love move,
and in its altering weather,
you two will turn away
as now you turn together"?

Is the ring given or lent? Does love ring round us,
or do we ring round it? Ring-giver, be warned.
Are you, in turn, expecting
love or the ring returned?

[*The New Yorker, February 9th, 1957*]

In Memory Of My Uncle Timothy

His name, they told me afterwards, was Able,
And he came, in yellow boots and a hat, and stood by
  the table
beside my Uncle Timmy, who went mad
later, and was a trouble to my Dad.
Uncle Tim said shakily "God, it's not you!"
but whoever he was, it was. So Tim took off his shoe,
shook it, and held it upside down. Out fell
a photograph of Grace, a sprig of fennel,
a bent crown piece, and a small gold key as well.
Tim spilt them in this man's lap, and he
—you'll not believe it—took out his eye
(glass, it was), and turned it over. On the back
was a crooked keyhole and a lock.
So he took Tim's key (he did, he did!)
and put it in. Up sprung a kind of lid.
He shoved it under Tim's nose. "Holy God!"
cried Tim. I looked, in the nick, before it closed.

Inside, upside down, was a tiny man
in a hat like Able's, with yellow boots on,
the spitting image of this living Able,
and there were Tim and me, upside down at the table,
and in the man's hand … but he quickly locked his eye,
tucking carefully away the key,
and put the thing crookedly back in his face,
gave Uncle the coin and the photograph of Grace,
stuck the sprig of fennel in his hat,
and off he went. "Uncle Tim" I cried, "what was that?"
I remember his face, but now I forget what he said.
Anyway, now Tim's dead.

Ghosts' Stories

That bull-necked blotch-faced farmer from Drumlore
would never dream (or so we heard him boast
to neighbours at the lamb sales in Kirkcudbright)
of paying the least attention to a ghost.

Were we to blame for teaching him a lesson?
We whored his daughter, spaded all his ewes,
brought a blight on his barley, drew the sea
rampaging over his sod ....

If we had any doubt that he deserved it,
that went when we heard him stamp his ruined acres
and blame it all on God.

When we went on and frightened Miss McQueen
for keeping children in on Halloween,
and wailed all night in the schoolhouse, she, poor woman,
sent for the Fire Brigade.
And so we made
fire lick from her hair, till they put her out.

The children knew what it was all about.

THE TALE THE HERMIT TOLD

It was one afternoon when I was young
in a village near here, which no one now remembers—
why, I will tell you—an afternoon of fiesta,
with the bells of the hermitage echoing in the mountains,
and a buzz of voices, and dogs barking. Some said
it could all be heard as far as Calatayud.
I was a boy then, though at that perilous point
when tiny things could terrify and amaze me.
The dust in the village square had been watered down,
and we waited, laughing and jostling
the satin rumps of the gipsy dancers.
Across from us, the girls, all lace and frills,
fluttered like tissue paper. Then at a signal,
as the charcoal-burner's dog rolled over and over,
shedding its ribbons, the village band
blundered into tune, and the day began.

    The dancing dizzied me. There was one gipsy
unlike the others, tall, who spun on her feet,
laughing to herself, lost in her own amazement.
I watched her as though in a dream. All round,
my uncles and other men were calling *olé*
while the women tittered and pouted.
There were more feet than shoes, more wine than glasses,
and more kisses than lips. The sun was burning.
Next came a magician, an ugly sly-eyed man

not from our district. "Fiesta, fiesta" he called,
then, chanting a kind of spell, he swore
he would conjure a live dove out of the air.
I saw the dove's wing peeping from his pocket,
so I wandered away, hating the sound of him,
among the tables, heavy with food and wine.
And there was the gipsy girl, standing alone,
head turned away to listen, as though she heard
bells in the hills. She saw me, and her eyes,
which were azure, not black, mocked me.
I could not stop looking. Lightly she danced across
and, keeping her eyes on mine, poured out
a glass of golden wine, and put it before me.

    I glanced from her eyes to the wine. In it, the sun
was a small gold coin, the people looked like nuts.
The band were brass buttons, the towering mountains
the size of pebbles, the houses, matchboxes
about the thumbnail square. A miniature magician
was letting loose a dove, which floated upwards,
and there, in that golden, glass-held afternoon,
were those mocking eyes. Time in that moment hung
upside down. In a gulp, I drank the wine.

    What happened next? You must listen.
Goggling boys, girls, dogs, band, gipsies, village,
dove, magician, all rolled down my throat.
Even the music glugged once and was gone.
I was standing nowhere, horrified, alone,
waiting for her eyes to appear and laugh
the afternoon back, but nothing moved or happened.
Nothing, nothing, nothing.

    All that night, I lay in a clump of pines
and seemed to hear the hunters with their dogs
(unribboned now) closing to flush me out.
I hid my face in the needles. All the next day,
I tried to wish the village back, to vomit

the wine, to free the white dove and the music.
I could not. And as time passed,
I lived on bitter nuts and bark and grasses,
And grew used to the woods. I am still here
on this barren mountainside. The years are nothing.
      Yet I am sure of this—
that somewhere in my body there is fiesta,
with ribboned dogs, balloons, and children dancing
in a lost village, that only I remember.
Often I have visions, and I hear
voices I know call out. Was it the false magician
who tempted me to magic? Or was it
the gipsy girl who dropped her eyes in a glass
and asked me to work wonders?
Even now, in age, I wait to see her,
still a girl, come spiralling through the woods,
bringing her mystery to me, and with her eyes
teaching me to undream myself, and be
a boy again, believing in a dove
made out of air, that circles overhead
on a lost afternoon of fiesta.

ODDMENTS, INKLINGS, OMENS, MOMENTS

Oddments, as when
you see through skin,
when flowers appear
to be eavesdropping,
or music somewhere
declares your mood;
when sleep fulfills
a feel of dying,
or fear makes ghosts
of clothes on a chair.

Inklings, as when
some room rhymes
with a lost time,
or a book reads
like a well-known dream;
when a smell recalls
portraits, funerals,
when a wish happens,
or a mirror sees
through distances.

Omens, as when
a shadow from nowhere
falls on a wall,

when a bird seems
to mimic your name,
when a cat eyes you
as though it knew,
and, heavy with augury,
a crow caws
cras cras from a tree.

Moments, as when
the air's awareness
makes guesses true,
when a hand's touch
speaks past speech,
or when, in poise,
two sympathies
lighten each other,
and love occurs
like song, like weather.

For Her Sake

Her world is all aware. She reads
omens in small happenings, the fall of a teaspoon,
flurries of birds, a cat's back arching,
words unspoken, wine spilt.
She will notice moods in handwriting,
be tuned to feelings in a room,
sense ill-luck in a house, take heed of ghosts,
hear children cry before the sound has reached her,
stay unperturbed in storms, keep silence
where speech would spoil. Days are her changes,
weather her time.

Whether it be becalmed in cool mornings
of air and water, or thunderstruck through nights
where flesh craves and is answered, in her, love
knows no division, is an incarnation
of all her wonder, as she makes
madness subside, and all thought-splintered things
grow whole again.

Look below. She walks in the garden,
preoccupied with paths, head bent,
beautiful, not at rest, as objects are,
but moving, in the fleck of light and shade.
Her ways are hers, not mine. Pointless to make

my sense of her, or claim her faithfulness.
She is as women are, aware
of her own mystery, in her way faithful
to flowers and days; and from the window's distance,
I watch her, haunted by her otherness.

Well to love true women, whose whims are wise,
whose world is warm, whose home is time,
and well to pleasure them, since, last of all,
they are the truth which men must tell,
and in their pleasure, houses lighten,
gardens grow faithful, and true tales are told.
Well to move from mind's distance
into their aura, where the air
is shifting, intimate, particular.

And of true women, she, whose eyes illumine
this day I wake in—well to mark
her weather, how her look is candid,
her voice clear-toned, her heart private,
her love both wild and reticent.
Well to praise and please her, well to make
this for her sake.

A Lesson For Beautiful Women

Gazing and gazing in the glass,
she might have noticed slow cotillions pass,
and might have seen
a blur of others in the antique green.
Transfixed instead,
she learned the inclinations of her neat small head,
and, startling her own surprise,
wondered at the wonder in her jewelled eyes.

Gardens of rainbow and russet might have caught her,
but, leaning over goldfish water,
she watched the red carp emphasise her mouth,
saw underneath
the long green weeds lace in
through a transparency of face and skin,
smiled at herself smiling reflectively,
lending a new complexion to the sky.

In service to her beauty,
long mornings lengthened to a duty
patiently served before the triple mirror
whose six eyes sent her many a time in terror
to hide in rows of whispering dresses;
but her small soul her own three goddesses
pursued, and if she turned away,

the same three mouths would breathe "Obey, obey!"

And in procession, young men princely came,
ambassadors to her cool perfect kingdom.
Given her distance by their praise,
she watched their unspeaking eyes adore her face.
Inside, her still self waited. Nothing moved.
Finally, by three husbands richly loved
(none of them young), she faded to her death,
the glass clouding with her last moist breath.

Mourned like a portrait, she was laid to rest;
and, left alone at last,
the small mim servant shuttered in her being
peeped mousily out; and seeing
the imperious mirrors glazed and still,
whimpered forlornly down the dark hall
"Oh, grieve for my body, who would not let me be.
She, not I, was a most beautiful lady."

[*The New Yorker, April 19th, 1958*]

SMALL SAD SONG

I am a lady
three feet small.
My voice is thin
but listen, listen.
Before I die
my modest death,
tell me what gentlemen
do with great ladies,
for thigh-high now
are the thoughts I think.

Once as a girl
I knew how to smile.
My world stayed small
as my playmates mountained.
My mother mocked me.
Dogs plagued me.
Now I am doomed
to dwell among elephants.
Sometimes I fall
in love with a bird.

I move amongst
donkeys and monkeys.

Dwarfs paw me
with stubby hands.
I cannot look at them.
There are no friends
of a suitable size.
Giants tease me.
Men do not choose me.
A hunchback loves me.

If someone moved me,
I might make
a monstrous poem,
huge as my dreams;
but what can come
from a thumbnail lady?
Words like watch-ticks,
whispers, twitterings,
suitable tinkles,
nothing at all.

[*The New Yorker, January 10th, 1959*]

OLD PAINTER TO YOUNG MODEL

If, when the paint has dried,
texture and tone deride
the image you would wear—
light in the eyes, loose fastening of hair—
forgive my error.
Read the face as mine,
my doom in colour and line,
my grief there, my terror.
To misunderstand
your face in my fashion
is my painter's passion.
I have lent you my rage.
Forgive my eyes their age.
Being seen is not seeing.
Forgive my wishful being
as I forgive you your youth.
My truth is not your truth.

Two Weathers

Tonight, the omens tell.
A lizard in the log
breaks for the chimney's shelter
at the first spurt of flame.
The gilded sea looks lucky,
and in the red-skied evening,
the swallows strake the eaves
where clouds of insects claim
tomorrow will be well.

Why should they run so counter,
outer and inner weather?
If all we felt were told
against this towering evening,
sky would go black,
swallows would screech and fall,
lizards devour the flowers,
and the fire ravish all,
with never a trace of gold.

CASA D'AMUNT

However gracefully
the spare leaves of the fig tree
in fullness overhead
with native courtesy
include us in their shade,
among the rented flowers
we keep a tenant's station.
The garden is not ours.

Under the arching trellis,
the gardener moves below.
Observe him on his knees
with offering of water
for roots that are not his,
tendering to a power
whose name he does not know,
but whom he must appease.

So do we too accord
the windings of the vine
and swelling of the olive
a serious mute oblation
and a respectful word,
aware of having put,
in spite of cultivation,
the worm within the fruit.

This garden tenancy
tests our habitual eye.
Now, water and the moon
join what we do not own.
The rent is paid in breath,
and so we freely give
the apple tree beneath
our unpossessive love.

Dear one, our present Eden
lays down this one condition:
we should not ask to wait.
No angel drives us out,
but time, without a word,
will show among the flowers,
sure as a flaming sword.
The garden is not ours.

[*The New Yorker, May 20th, 1967*]

LIVING IN TIME

This morning, overpowered
by weather and discontent,
I climb the escarpment
and manage to be lost
in watching for an hour

the pointlessness of swallows
which have nothing to do with me
larruping through the trees,
and in curling thrown stones
into the dull valley.

Yet on my slow way home,
the dark selves from the study
fall into step beside me
and one by one resume
the morning's lame conundrum.

Bird-minded now, I answer
loosely, light-heartedly,
but their presences tower.
Looking becomes a question.
Thought glooms the day.

Then, unexpectedly,
she is waiting in the doorway,

ready with something to say,
so much herself, so beautifully
occupying her body

that I am all wonder,
beyond mind and words.
She wears the day about her.
The dark ones disappear, and birds
reclaim the particular air.

Better to live in time.
The moment is her home.
Better to leave it
as something that is, that happens
as luck will have it.

[*The New Yorker, February 1st, 1959*]

A Leavetaking

What a day we parted on!
Sludge. Not a wink of sun.
Heavy headlines, traffic breakdowns.
Three damp children dressed as clowns.
A sobbing drunk on the corner, reeling.
The sky as smoke-stained as a ceiling.
Any two but she and I
would have been glad to say good-bye.
The houses bowed their heads in rows
as, with rain running down my nose,
I watched her go her ways,
a bright true tear across a dirty face.

A HOMECOMING

Landfall in Ithaca. And so, Ulysses,
the will to win was all, all wandering done.
It did not matter what the past had cost
as now in your great bed you drowned again.
Gone were the various trials by sea, and gone
the trials by women—nights of sweated lust
in Circe's bed, the Sirens' dreamed-of kisses,
white-limbed Nausicaa—all past, all lost.
The Suitors? Who could expect you to be just?
Outside, the heaped-up bodies of the slain
slopped in their blood. But at your side lay she,
your virtuous weeping queen, Penelope.

She was good, she was true. Why then did you choose
        to carve
so cruel a way back to your marriage-bed?
What was there to avenge? Not faithlessness,
as all your baffling arrows found their dead?
Yet did her weaving and unweaving ask
so liberal a testament of blood?
What then? Was she too good to be true?
Did it come back, the phantom of your lust,
to haunt the restless edges of your sleep,
whispering "Are these faithful tears for you,
or in the web of darkness does she weep
for silent bloodstained lips, for the still thighs
of all the dead, for silver-tongued Eurymachus,
for Antinous, your arrow in his throat,
for Polybus, whose spilt blood fills his eyes?"
Was it this, Ulysses? And from some remote
lost island in the dark, did you cry at last
"O doubt, O doubt, O all the bitter past!"

Childhood Landscape

In green corners,
dark glens, valleys
which a wood edges
and no road touches,
always one house,
withdrawn, white,
one window alight.

And passing, I wonder
idly, uneasily,
who could be there—
farmers, gentry,
laughing, meeting—
and what might grant me
the right of entry?

No one, nothing.
The mind, once freed,
grasps at such lights
with a child's greed,
wistfully claiming
lost prerogatives
of homecoming.

SPAIN, MORNING

Up early, out of a dream
of tall perplexing women.
Warm on the terrace, with sun
staining the clumsy town.
Spanish, in children's voices,
and olive trees and sea
fasten the day down
and tell me where I am.

A cock crows its alarm.
Turkeys cluck in the rubble.
The children, drowsed and warm,
trail to the breakfast table,
to grapes and figs in season.
The dream dies down,
and I wonder in the sun
what to make of the morning.

To see if I am the same,
I speak, in my own voice,
an answer which satisfies
something the children ask,
and go to my blank desk,
balancing day and dream,
to see what light will come
with the help of a lucky rhyme
or a word in the right quarter.

[*The Atlantic, November 1st, 1958*]

A NOTE FROM THE COAST

This coast's not
easy in winter.
The sky's unkindly
gray. The seamen
grump in their boots.
The ferry takes
too long to turn,
and when you put
a foot on the island,
there are no children
calling hello.
So, if you come,
come in the dark,
bring warm clothes,
and don't expect
me to be easy.
I'll have had
my eyes on the ice,
and won't be used
to your words and ways.
Yet out tonight
there's veering wind
and a smoor on the sea.
Soon, the geese
should be crossing the moon,
so come, but take
your time and my time.
I'll bring the boat,
but let us meet
gently, gently.
This coast is not
ours in winter.

[*The New Yorker, December15th, 1956*]

L'amour De Moi

The tune at first is odd, though still familiar.
It asks and answers, as you hear
the children playing it on their thin recorders
over and over, in the afternoon,
through breath and error, with the huge blue day
hovering overhead. The house dozes,
and guests asleep—uncles, grandmothers, cousins—
accept it easily into their dreams,
like repetitions of the same cool breeze,
and sigh. The notes, brief moths among the roses,
falter but do not fall. A wind passes,
and then the tune again, the first phrase firm,
the second wavering and fanciful,
the last settling, as the air falls still.

Later, at night, its counterpoint—
the family after dinner, lifting down
instruments from the walls, and their huge shadows
huddled, bending together, as candle flames
waver with the first enquiring chord.
Uncles, cousins, friends—they yield to the air,
subscribed by lifting strings and the bland oboe,
gloom of the cello, thump of drum.
The children turn in sleep upstairs, dreaming
in waves that widen from their own small music—
heartbeat and breath, the fanciful lift of fiddles,
the falling arm, the last cool phrase, falling.
Shadows pause in their place. Outside,
the garden breathes beneath suspended stars.

This is true harmony, and in this tune
turn families, passions, histories, planets, all.

PIGEONS

On the crooked arm of Columbus, on his cloak,
they mimic his blind and statuary stare,
and the chipped profiles of his handmaidens
they adorn with droppings. Over the loud square,
from all the arms and ledges of their rest,
only a bread crust or a bell unshelves them.
Adding to Atlas' globe, they dispose themselves
with a fat propriety, and pose as garlands
importantly about his burdened shoulders.
Occasionally a lift of wind uncarves them.

　Stone becomes them; they, in their turn, become it.
Their opal eyes have a monumental cast.
And, in a maze of noise,
their quiet *croomb croomb* dignifies the spaces,
suggesting the sound of silence. On cobbled islands,
marooned in tantrums of traffic, they know their place,
faithful and anonymous, like servants,
and never beg, but properly receive.

　Arriving in rainbows of oil-and-water feathers,
they fountain down from buttresses and outcrops,
from Fontainebleau and London,
and, squat on the margins of roofs, with a gargoyle look,
they note, from an edge of air, with hooded eyes,
the city slowly lessening the sky.

All praise to them who nightly in the parks
keep peace for us; who, cosmopolitan,
patrol and people all cathedraled places,
and easily, lazily haunt and inhabit
St. Paul's, St. Peter's, or the Madeleine,
the paved courts of the past, pompous as keepers—
a sober race of messengers and custodians,
neat in their international uniforms,
alighting with a word perhaps from Rome.
Permanence is their business, space and time
their special preservations; and wherever
the great stone men we save from death are stationed,
appropriately on the head of each is perched,
as though for ever, his appointed pigeon.

[*The New Yorker, November 13th, 1954*]

WHAT'S WHAT

Most people know
the story of how
the frog was a prince
and the dragon was ticklish,
or how the princess
grew fat in the end;
nevertheless,
think of the chance
that the youngest son took—
gloom to the left of him,
groans to the right of him,
no spell to tell him
which way to take,
no map, no book,
no real interest.
All he could say was
"maybe I'm me,"
but he knew not to trust
the wizards who seemed,
the bird with the breast
of too many colours,
the princess who hummed
too perfect a song.
The going was not good,
but his curious head

said over and over
ridiculous words
like *quince* and *Fray Bentos*
all through the wood.

"Yes," he said firmly,
"nobody pays me,
nobody knows me,
so I will decide
which tree will amaze me
when I see a leaf
I can be sure of.
Whom do I listen to?
Not that toad
with the gem in its head,
nor that mole that mumbles
precise directions,
nor the nice wizard,
so soft and helpful,
nor sweet old women
gathering faggots.
It's that clumsy bird
who looks away,
with only one eye—
untidy feathers,
flying absent-mindedly,
out in all weathers,
little to say—
he's for me.
He's not after
a cut of the treasure.
He knows well
that he's going nowhere
and, what's more,
he doesn't care.

If I'd listened to wizards
and looked in crystals,
I'd be expert
at going wrong;
but I know my birdsong.
Hearing his *tip-tippy*,
I know who *he* is.
I'll go *his* way.

Needless to say,
the youngest son won
with enough to go on;
and the one-eyed bird,
whoever he was,
went *tip-tip-tippy*
to pleasure his own
well-worn feathers,
over and over,
with no one to hear …

Then, one day,
the youngest son
had a youngest son,
and so on.

[*The New Yorker, December 7th, 1957*]

From PASSWORDS

1963

FOREIGNERS

Owls, like monks of a rare, feathered order,
haunt one aloof, lopped tower in this
unlikely city, cresting the broken stones
like ghosts at dusk, watchful, wary,
describing soft, slow curves in the failing sky.

Supremely odd and patiently oblivious
to all but wind and owlhood, they tatter
the evening air with their broad, sooty wings.
And over all, the tower seems content
with its alien colony. For whose is a city?

Yet below, the jabbering birds of the sprawled suburbs
complain from the lower roofs, look up from crusts
and blame owls for the dust, for all the dismal
workaday winging. The atmosphere is crowded,
to their native eyes, with a woeful weight of owls.

Natural enough, their twitterings. They were there
first, they cleared the air and made
nests in new places, scraped for straws, foraged
for food, grew ancestors and histories.
Now come the owls, a late, impervious entry.

What do the owls answer? To wit, nothing.
And sure enough, with time passing, the tower
becomes a landmark, mentioned in the guidebooks,
with owls as appropriate appendages. The city
absorbs them into its anonymous air.

Now, other birds alight on the battlements,
occasionally singing. Not worthwhile to war
over a lack of crumbs, in alien weather.
Who gives a hoot, say owls. The wind is common.
Let all poor birds be brothers under the feather.

[*The Atlantic, October 1st, 1962*]

DISGUISES

My selves, my presences,
like uniforms and suits,
some stiff, some soiled, some threadbare,
and not all easy-fitting,
hang somewhere in the house.

A friend or a misfortune
will force me, on occasion,
into a sober habit,
uncomfortably formal,
in keeping, though unwise.

But otherwise I wear
something old and easy,
with little thought to please,
nor a glance in the mirror,
nor a care for size;

being caught, in consequence,
sporting the wrong colour
in appropriate weather—
odd shirts, uneven socks,
and most unsuitable ties.

I should have a tailor,
or, failing him, a mirror;
but being possessed of neither,
I sit in my stubborn skin and count
all clothing as disguise.

[*The New Yorker, September 3rd, 1960;*
The Atlantic, June 1st, 1962]

SPEAKING A FOREIGN LANGUAGE

How clumsy on the tongue, these acquired idioms,
after the innuendoes of our own. How far
we are from foreigners, what faith
we rest in one sentence, hoping a smile will follow
on the appropriate face, always wallowing
between what we long to say and what we can,
trusting the phrase is suitable to the occasion,
the accent passable, the smile real,
always asking the traveller's fearful question—
    what is being lost in translation?

Something, to be sure. And yet, to hear
the stumbling of foreign friends, how little we care
for the wreckage of word or tense. How endearing they are,
and how our speech reaches out, like a helping hand,
or limps in sympathy. Easy to understand,
through the tangle of language, the heart behind
groping toward us—to make the translation of
    syntax into love.

THE SYNTAX OF SEASONS

Autumn was adjectival. I recall
a gray, dank, gnarled spell
when all wore fall-quality, a bare
mutating atmosphere.

Winter hardened into nouns. Withdrawn
in lamplight, I would crown
the cold with thought-exactitude, would claim
the drear air with a name.

In spring, all language loosened and became
less in demand, limping, lame,
faced with the bursting days. What told
was tongue-tied wonder at the green and gold.

Steeped now in summer, though our chattering
rises and falls, occasional as birdsong,
we fall to silence under the burning sun,
and feel the great verbs run.

[*The Atlantic, August 1st, 1962*]

The Figures On The Frieze

Darkness wears off, and, dawning into light,
they find themselves unmagically together.
He sees the stains of morning in her face.
She shivers, distant in his bitter weather.

Diminishing of legend sets him brooding.
Great goddess-figures conjured from his book
blur what he sees with bafflement of wishing.
Sulky, she feels his fierce, accusing look.

Familiar as her own, his body's landscape
seems harsh and full to her habitual eyes.
Mystery leaves, and, mercilessly flying,
the blind fiends come, emboldened by her cries.

Avoiding simple reach of hand for hand
(which would surrender pride) by noon they stand
withdrawn from touch, reproachfully alone,
small in each other's eyes, tall in their own.

Wild with their misery, they entangle now
in baffling agonies of why and how.
Afternoon glimmers, and they wound anew,
flesh, nerve, bone, gristle in each other's view.

"What have you done to me?" From each proud heart,
new phantoms walk in the deceiving air.
As the light fails, each is consumed apart,
he by his ogre vision, she by her fire.

When night falls, out of a despair of daylight,
they strike the lying attitudes of love,
and through the perturbations of their bodies,
each feels the amazing, murderous legends move.

[*The New Yorker, February 9th, 1963*]

OUTLOOK, UNCERTAIN

No season
brings conclusion.

Each year,
through heartache, nightmare,

true loves alter,
marriages falter,

and lovers illumine
the antique design,

apart, together,
foolish as weather,

right as rain,
sure as ruin.

Must you, then, and I
adjust the whole sky

over every morning;
or else, submitting

to cloud and storm;
enact the same

lugubrious ending,
new lives pending?

[*The Atlantic, October 1st, 1959*]

Me To You

Summer's gone brown, and, with it,
our wanderings in the shires, our ways.
Look at us now.
A shuttered house drips in Moroccan rain.
A mill sits ghostly in the green of France.
Beaches are empty now of all but pebbles.
But still, at crossroads, in senorial gardens,
we meet, sleep, wrangle, part, meet, part,
making a lodging of the heart.

Now that the sea begins to dull with winter,
and I so far, and you so far,
(and home further than either),
write me a long letter,
as if from home.
        Tell me about the snowfalls
at night, and tell me how we'd sit in firelight,
hearing dogs huff in sleep, hearing the geese
hiss in the barn, hearing the horse clop home.
Say how the waterfall sounds, and how the weeds
trail in the slithering river.
Write me about the weather.

Perhaps
a letter across water,
something like this, but better,
would almost take us strangely
closer to home.

Write, and I'll come.

[*The New Yorker, January 19th 1963*]

The O-Filler

One noon in the library, I watched a man—
imagine!—filling in O's, a little, rumpled
nobody of a man, who licked his stub of pencil
and leaned over every O with a loving care,
shading it neatly, exactly to its edges,
until the open pages
were pocked and dotted with solid O's, like villages
and capitals on a map. And yet, so peppered,
somehow the book looked lived in and complete.

That whole afternoon, as the light outside softened,
and the library groaned woodenly,
he worked and worked, his O-so-patient shading
descending like an eyelid over each open O
for page after page. Not once did he miss one,
or hover even a moment over an *a*,
or an *e* or a *p* or a *g*. Only the O's—
oodles of O's, O's multitudinous, O's manifold,
O's italic and roman.
And what light on his crumpled face when he discovered—
as I supposed—odd words like *zoo* and *ooze*,
polo, oolong and *odontology*!

Think now. In that limitless library,
all round the steep-shelved walls, bulging in their bindings,
books stood, waiting. Heaven knows how many

he had so far filled, but no matter, there still were
uncountable volumes of O-laden prose, and odes
with inflated capital O's (in the manner of Shelley),
O-bearing Bibles and biographies,
even whole sections devoted to O alone,
all his for the filling. Glory, glory, glory!
How lovely and open and endless the world must
    have seemed to him,
how utterly clear-cut! Think of it. A pencil
was all he needed. Life was one wide O.

    Anyway, why in the end should O's not be closed
as eyes are? I envied him. After all,
sitting across from him, had I accomplished
anything as firm as he had, or as fruitful?
What could I show? A handful of scrawled lines,
an afternoon yawned and wondered away,
and a growing realization that in time
even my scribbled words would come
under his grubby thumb, and the blinds be drawn
on all my O's. And only this thought for comfort—
that when he comes to this poem, a proper joy
may amaze his wizened face, and, O, a pure pleasure
make his meticulous pencil quiver.

[*The New Yorker, February 1st, 1960*]

Curiosity
(for M. M-M)

may have killed the cat; more likely
the cat was just unlucky, or else curious
to see what death was like, having no cause
to go on licking paws, or fathering
litter on litter of kittens, predictably.

   Nevertheless, to be curious
is dangerous enough. To distrust
what is always said, what seems,
to ask odd questions, interfere in dreams,
leave home, smell rats, have hunches
does not endear him to those doggy circles
where well-smelt baskets, suitable wives, good lunches
are the order of things, and where prevails
much wagging of incurious heads and tails.

   Face it. Curiosity
will not cause him to die—
only lack of it will.
Never to want to see
the other side of the hill,
or that improbable country
where living is an idyll
(although a probable hell)

would kill us all.
Only the curious
have, if they live, a tale
worth telling at all.

   Dogs say he loves too much, is irresponsible,
is changeable, marries too many wives,
deserts his children, chills all dinner tables
with tales of his nine lives.
Well, he is lucky. Let him be
nine-lived and contradictory,
curious enough to change, prepared to pay
the cat price, which is to die
and die again and again,
each time with no less pain.
A cat minority of one
is all that can be counted on
to tell the truth. And what he has to tell
on each return from hell
is this: that dying is what the living do,
that dying is what the loving do,
and that dead dogs are those who do not know
that dying is what, to live, each has to do.

[*The New Yorker, November 14th, 1959*]

137

PROPINQUITY

is the province of cats. Living by accident,
lapping the food at hand, or sleeking down
in an adjacent lap when sleep occurs to them,
never aspiring to consistency
in homes or partners, unaware of property,
cats take their chances, love by need and nearness
as long as the need lasts, as long as the nearness
is near enough. The code of cats is simply
to take what comes. And those poor souls who claim
to own a cat, who long to recognize
in bland and narrowing eyes a look like love,
are bound to suffer should they expect
cats to come purring punctually home.
Home is only where the food and the fire are,
but might be anywhere. Cats fall on their feet,
nurse their own wounds, attend to their own laundry,
and purr at appropriate times. O folly, folly
to love a cat, and yet
we dress with love the distance that they keep,
the hair-raising way they have, and easily blame
all the abandoned litters and torn ears
on some marauding tiger. Well, no matter;
cats do not care.
   Yet part of us is cat. Confess—
love turns on accident, and needs

nearness; and the various selves we have
all come from our cat-wanderings, our chance
crossings. Imagination prowls at night,
cat-like among odd possibilities.
Only our dog-sense brings us faithfully homeward,
makes meaning out of accident, keeps faith,
and, cat-and-dog, the arguments go at it.
But every night, outside, cat-voices call
us out to take a chance, to leave
the safety of our blankets, and to let
what happens, happen. "Live, live!" they catcall.
"Each moment is your next! Propinquity,
propinquity is all!"

[*The New Yorker, January 14th, 1961*]

FROG DREAM

Nightlong, frogs in the pool
croak out calamity till, wakeful,
I interpret each crooked syllable.

The sound is churlish, coarse—
frog notes grating out a hoarse
chorus of slow remorse,

as I do, in half-sleep,
until, drifting, I cannot keep
the dark from deepening,

or dream voices from becoming
peepers and grunters, churning
my madness over. The pool is lapping,

weed-streaked, in my head.
Frogs echo from the edges of the bed,
in the grieving voices of the long dead,

grudges long hidden in their old throats,
hauntings, water horror, hates.
Somewhere, shivering, daylight waits.

Later, I wake, in the sanity of dawn,
and walk to the pool, glassy under the sun.
What did I dream? The frogs have all gone down.

[*The Atlantic, August 1st, 1959*]

WISHES

Sudden silence, an angel passing over,
two saying the same word, simultaneously,
a star falling, the first fruit of the year,
the breastbone of the chicken, scraped and dry—
each an occasion to wish on, a wish given.

Easy enough for children, for whom to wish
is only a way of bringing a party closer
or acquiring pennies or cake, and for whose sake
we attend to teeth beneath stones and believe in magic,
not indulgently but somehow because
each time the silver coin appears where the tooth was,
the party seems quick in coming, and beggars ride
pell-mell over the countryside.

But for ourselves, with fewer teeth and no faith
in miracles or good angels, a falling star
is likely to be uncomfortable. Oh, we can ask for
new lives, more money, or a change of face,
but hardly seriously. The heart is lacking.
We know too much, and wishing smacks of daydream
and discontent—not magic. Anyway, we are wary
of strings and snags or, worse, that, once fulfilled,
the thing we wished for might be old and cold.

Yet still the children come, with serious
rapt faces, offering us wishes.
Take this wishbone, delicate where the breast was,
whitened now by the sun, stick-brittle.

Hold one stem of it, lightly, with your little
finger. I will hold the other.
Now make your wish, my love; but never tell.

And I? I always wish you well;
but here, in this poise before the fruit can fall,
or the star burn out, or the word dwindle,
before the hovering angel
flies out of mind, before the bone is broken,
I wish we wish the same wish, the unspoken.

[*The New Yorker, November 11th, 1961*]

What Bones Say

The skeleton
is hardly a lesson
in human nature.

Similarly, stones
are the bones of landscapes,
and yet trees blossom

in contradiction.
We are much more
than our brittle topography.

Nevertheless,
what is it
about bones and skull

that suggests a whole
compelling humanity?
The bones' statuary

pose, like handwriting,
the thin, helpless,
scrawled mortality?

Wise to keep

a skull in the cupboard,
not as warning

but as a bulwark
against disaster
or wild dreaming.

And you—it behooves you,
that you may dispense
with my passing madness,

to take fair note
of this ultimate:
a skeleton loves you.

[*The New Yorker, May 27th, 1961*]

A Lesson In Music

Play the tune again; but this time
with more regard for the movement at the source of it,
and less attention to time. Time falls
curiously in the course of it.

Play the tune again; not watching
your fingering, but forgetting, letting flow
the sound till it surrounds you. Do not count
or even think. Let go.

Play the tune again; but try to be
nobody, nothing, as though the pace
of the sound were your heart beating, as though
the music were your face.

Play the tune again. It should be easier
to think less every time of the notes, of the measure.
It is all an arrangement of silence. Be silent, and then
play it for your pleasure.

Play the tune again; and this time, when it ends,
do not ask me what I think. Feel what is happening
strangely in the room as the sound glooms over
you, me, everything.

Now,
play the tune again.

[*The Atlantic, March 1st, 1958*]

THE SPIRAL

The seasons of this year are in my luggage.
Now, lifting the last picture from the wall,
I close the eyes of the room. Each footfall
clatters on the bareness of the stair.
The family ghosts fade in the hanging air.
Mirrors reflect the silence. There is no message.
I wait in the still hall for a car to come.
Behind, the house will dwindle to a name.

Places, addresses, faces left behind.
The present is a devious wind
obliterating days and promises.
Tomorrow is a tinker's guess.
Marooned in cities, dreaming of greenness,
or dazed by journeys, dreading to arrive—
change, change is where I live.

For possibility,
I choose to leave behind
each language, each country.
Will this place be an end,
or will there be one other,
truer, rarer?

Often now, in dream,
abandoned landscapes come,

figuring a constant theme:
Have you left us behind?
What have you still to find?

Across the spiral distance,
through time and turbulence,
the rooted self in me
maps out its true country.

And, as my father found
his own small weathered island,
so will I come to ground

where that small man, my son,
can put his years on.

For him, too, time will turn.

[*The New Yorker, April 6th, 1963*]

From WEATHERING

1978

THE MANSE

The house that shored my childhood up
razed to the ground? I stood, amazed,
gawking at a block of air,
unremarkable except
I had hung it once with crazy
daywish and nightmare.

Expecting to pass a wistful
indulgent morning, I had sprung the gate.
Facing me was a wood
between which and myself
a whole crow-gabled and slated
mythology should have stood.

No room now for the rambling
wry remembering I had planned;
nor could I replant
that plot with a second childhood.
Luck, to have been handed
instead a forgettable element,

and not to have had to meet
regretful ghosts in rooms of glass.
That house by now is fairytale
and I can gloss it over
as easily as passing
clear through a wall.

AUNT ELSIE

Aunt Elsie, who is ninety,
and delicate as eggshell,
mistakes me for my father,
talks to my son as me;
pours tea with knitting fingers
into a brittle cup
and asks me what I plan to do
when I grow up.

I ask myself, Aunt Elsie,
questions much the same,
and wonder at the easy way
you handle time,
especially when I sit between
my father and my son,
fastened to both dimensions,
father and son in one.

You have arrived, Aunt Elsie,
at where confusion ends,
in that astonished present
where time unwinds,
where what you will can happen in
the compass of your chair
at a flick of your silk handkerchief
into the crowded air.

Questions of who we are
should never have an answer.
We leave old selves, like places,
disquietingly behind.
And as for the complexities
we fail to understand,
at least they make their sense in
Aunt Elsie's scrapbook mind.

My Father, Dying

At summer's succulent end,
the house is green-stained.
I reach for my father's hand

and study his ancient nails.
Feeble-bodied, yet at intervals
a sweetness appears and prevails.

The heavy-scented night
seems to get at his throat.
It is as if the dark coughed.

In the other rooms of the house,
the furniture stands mumchance.
Age has engraved his face.

Cradling his wagged-out chin,
I shave him, feeling bone
stretching the waxed skin.

By his bed, the newspaper lies furled.
He has grown too old
to unfold the world,

which has dwindled to the size of a sheet.
His room has a stillness to it.
I do not call it waiting, but I wait,

anxious in the dark, to see if
the butterfly of his breath
has fluttered clear of death.

There is so much might be said,

dear old man, before I find you dead;
but we have become too separate

now in human time
to unravel all the interim
as your memory goes numb.

But there is no need for you to tell—
no words, no wise counsel,
no talk of dying well.

We have become mostly hands
and voices in your understanding.
The whole household is pending.

I am not ready
to be without your frail and wasted body,
your miscellaneous mind-way,

the faltering vein of your life.
Each evening, I am loathe
to leave you to your death.

Nor will I dwell on
the endless, cumulative question
I ask, being your son.

But on any one
of these nights soon,
for you, the dark will not crack with dawn,

and then I will begin
with you that hesitant conversation
going on and on and on.

[*The New Yorker, November 16th, 1976*]

A Day For The Book

It was a day from a book,
steeped in its own warm juice,
heavy with smells of growing,
a day the early summer
sent to confirm its coming,
laburnum and hornbeam
bartering yellow and green.

I took
the chance that you that day were ready to take
the chance. The chance was taken,
that eye-taut silence broken.

I remember the sun on your skin
till it seemed light-thin.
I remember going in, in
to the waters of your eyes,
reflecting the sky-blue look
of the lake, with a swallow or two
cutting the air in arcs.
What was said could never be true,
told as it was in time,
but the day was true.

It is a day in a book
now, as I turn it over,
not thinking to tie it in
to any before or after.
I remember, the fire lit,
you saying something like that
and the smoke fuming out
just as you spoke.

These words are something like smoke.

Me To You (1 & 2)

I

Summer's gone brown and, with it,
our wanderings in the shires, our ways.
Look at us now.
A shuttered house drips in Moroccan rain.
A mill sits ghostly in the green of France.

Beaches are empty now of all but pebbles.
But still, at crossroads, in senorial gardens,
we meet, sleep, wrangle, part, meet, part,
making a lodging of the heart.

Now that the sea begins to dull with winter,
and I so far, and you so far
(and home further than either),
write me a long letter,
as if from home.
     Tell me about the snowfalls
at night, and tell me how we'd sit in firelight,
hearing dogs huff in sleep, hearing the geese
hiss in the barn, hearing the horse clop home.
Say how the waterfall sounds, and how the weeds
trail in the slithering river.
Write me about the weather.

Perhaps
a letter across water,
something like this, but better,
would almost move us strangely
closer to home.

Write, and I'll come.

II

All day I have been writing you a letter.

Now, after hours of gazing at the page
and watching the screen of rain, I have enacted
a flow of endless letters in my head
(all of them different) and not one
in any written shape to send.
Those letters never end.

In between pages of wishing, I walked to the river
and wrote you of how the water
wrinkles and eddies and wanders away.
That was easier to say.

I wrote of how the snow
had fallen and turned blue,
and how the bush you wanted
could not be planted.

Some pages were all remembering—the places,
faces, frontiers, rooms, and days we went through
ages ago.
(Do you do this too?)
Always coming back to snow.

Mostly an endless, useless run of questions.
How are you now? How is it there?
Who will you and I
be in a year?
Who are we now?

Oh no,
there is no letter to send you, only this stream
of disconnected brooding, this rhythm
of wanting, cumbersome
in words, lame.

Come.

QUARRELS

I can feel a quarrel blowing up in your body,
as old salts can smell storms
which are still fretting under the horizon,
before your eyes have flashed their first alarms.

Whatever the reason, the reason is not the reason.
It's a weather. It's a wellhead about to blaze gas,
flaring up when you suddenly stumble over
an alien presence in your private space.

You face me, eyes slitted like a cat's.
I can feel your nails uncurling.
The tendons in your neck twang with anger.
Your face is liquid as it is in loving.

Marking how often you say "always" and "never",
I on my side grow icy, tall, and thin
until, with watching you, I forget to listen,
and am burned through and through with your high
passion.

Face to face, like wrestlers or lovers,
we spit it out. Your words nip, like bites.
Your argument's a small, tenacious creature
I try to stomp on with great logical boots.

Dear angry one, let the boots and the skittering beast
chase wildly round the room like Tom and Jerry
or who and why. Let us withdraw and watch them,
but side by side, not nose to nose and wary.

That is the only way we'll disentangle
the quarrel from ourselves and switch it off.
Not face to face. The sparks of confrontation
too easily ignite a rage like love.

The he-with-her subsides, the I-with-you
looms into place. So we fold up the words
and, with a movement much like waking up,
we turn the weather down, and turn towards.

MARCH

An ill-starred month, this was.
I found the slate-gray vase,
once bargained for in Corinth,
in shards on the stone floor.
No, gasped the wide-eyed maid,
it must have been the wind.

The weather spelt disquiet -
changeable, indecisive.
We did not sleep but dozed
on the edge of bad dreams.
Nothing was what it seemed.

Words came in fits and starts.
The animals were jumpy.
We moved uneasily about the room.
A distant uncle died, in gloom.

The vase is dust and past.
Pointless to blame the wind
or the bland gray-eyed maid.

You wept once in your sleep.
Those were bad times for us to keep.

An ill-starred month, it was.

SCOTLAND

It was a day peculiar to this piece of the planet,
when larks rose on long thin strings of singing
and the air shifted with the shimmer of actual angels.
Greenness entered the body. The grasses
shivered with presences, and sunlight
stayed like a halo on hair and heather and hills.
Walking in town, I saw, in a radiant raincoat,
the woman from the fish-shop. "What a day it is!"
cried I, like a sunstruck madman.
And what did she have to say for it?
Her brow grew bleak, her ancestors raged in their graves
as she spoke with their ancient misery:
"We'll pay for it, we'll pay for it, we'll pay for it!"

GALILEA

Bleached white, bedazzled
by the bright light falling,
the hilltop holds me up.
Below, the coastline bares its teeth.

Winded, burned to the bone, between
the stony green of the olive,
the gray grimace of stone,
I look dazedly down.

How to come to rest
in this raw, whittled landscape
where earth, air, fire, and water
bluntly demand obeisance?

Perhaps to fix one place
in a shifting world where time
talks and where too many selves
criss-cross and demand
enactment and re-enactment,

somewhere decent to die in,
somewhere which could become
landscape and vocabulary,
equilibrium, home.

New York Surprised

I come down suddenly, out of the sky,
into this city, which I knew
well enough once to move about in by instinct.

Not now. Not now.

From the taxi window, I worry that signs, wondering
whether or not the driver knows his way
to the house I hope to be in, to the ones
whose letters said "Come" when I read them
on a stone bench in the garden,
twelve droning Spanish hours away.
Of course he knows his way,
but nevertheless I worry.

"There are too many people in the world,"
the old postman would mumble, as he thumbed
my letters out, smelling of sweat and donkeys.

There are too many people, I say to myself anxiously.
There were too many people before, in the afternoons here
when the spring was sweet like this one, when the sun
splattered on unexpected pinks and windows
flaming, when I knew
where everyone was, when the houses

stood still in their places,
when I knew how long to wait for the door to click,
when to go home, when to be alone,
when to say "Yes" and be sure.

Newly arrived from nowhere,
where the only movement has been
in leaves, in water running, in the slow
flow of the day, with odd words jotted down
to hold a moment, to tell time in a letter,
I watch the towers close in and the city
awe me with windows. I nibble my nails
away with unknowing. Who will be there?
Which me will I meet from the past in the towering city
I once knew as I know
now the ways of almonds and mimosa
in the village in which I never
arrive but always am?

Only my name is the same.

[*The New Yorker, April 6th, 1966*]

In Mexico

Water mirrors the huge
silk handkerchief of the sky.

Dipping the cup of my fingers
into the eye of the well,
I drink to the day. The water
runs like an answer down my throat,
as my hands are making ancient prayers.

Isla Negra, Chile

Sitting with the Pacific between my toes
in Chile, which I only knew by name,
in Isla Negra, which is not an island,
I listen across amazement to a girl
punctuating the air on a guitar.

There are places too well known to notice
and places unimaginable like dreams.
I am
suspended between the two. I know the sun
of old. I know the sea, over and over,
and once again. I do not know the girl
except by touch. The moment has no name.
After three playings, I will know the tune.

TIREE

Over the walking foreshore cluttered
black with the tide's untidy wrack,
and pools that brimmed with the moon,
I trespassed underwater.
My feet found seabed sand.
The night wore guilt like a watermark
and down the guilty dark,
the gulls muttered to windward.
Far out, the tide spoke back.

Across the morning clean of my walking
ghost and the driftwood litter,
singly I walked into singing light.

The rocks walked light on the water,
and clouds as clean as spinnakers
puffed in the sea-blue sky.
A starfish signed the sand. Beyond,
I faced the innocent sea.

CHELSEA REACH

The boat rides watertight, moored, fog-shrouded.
The boy reads, floats, daydreams.
With less daylight, I get to know darkness.

Rueful winter, laying gloom on the river.
Unkind winter, contradictor of comfort.
Blank winter, an unmarked blackboard.

Evenings abroad are longer, with more remembering.
Conclusions break, a long slow march of thought.
I sit in the lamp's pool, my head in darkness.

The boy mutters lost words, the phrases of dreams.
The tide laps him to sleep, nudges him with morning.
He rises, born and beginning. To watch him is wonder.

That might be enough, the hollow hull-shelter
shrouded in winter, shipshape on the river,
the boy bright with questions, I fathering answer

but for the gathering gloom, the looming winter,
the present light breaking, change making fear,
tide on gray tide, another, another, another.

[*The New Yorker, February 6th, 1971*]

Geneva

In this town, in the blurred and snowy dawn,
under humped eaves, in a lopsided house
built, it would seem, by gnomes, in the first
hushed snowlight, in the snowy hush,
an alarm clock catches and trills time on its tongue
like a clockwork rooster. Silence. And then another
begins to burr in the attic, its small bell
nibbling at the edges of awareness.
So the day speaks. Sleep is left like fallen snow
on the tumbled snow-white bed in which we wake.
    And then the bells begin their wrangling preamble
to the hour, giving tongue, tumbling
one over the other, faltering, failing, falling
like snow on the white pillow. Their gold tongues wag
with time. (They are rung, it would seem, by gnomes).
Now, in the town, the day is on its way.
    Snowfalls nibble at the windows. In the great
assembly halls, bells ring
along the marble lobbies, calling the delegates in
to the long tables of words where, crouched
like watchmakers, they worry away
the agendas of the world, their tongues ticking
like mechanisms, and in the earphones
the voices of interpreters trill their small alarms.
    Time, gentlemen. Time is what they are telling.

The snow melts silently, the watchsprings twitter.
What was the question? Bells
telling time obscure the answer.
(The clocks never need translation.)
Eyes on the snow, we listen.
The words roll on like bells
marking time; they fall and drift like snow,
leaving their meaning in a watery
residue. The diplomats pace the halls,
watching the clock, attentive to alarms.
    All these words telling time fall thick as snowflakes.
We hope for a conclusion from the clock,
which never comes, except in intervals
of snowy silence. Clocks obscure our time.
    Now, in the town, something is ticking away.
(Gnomes can be glimpsed at night, in pools of lamplight,
peering through glass at something small and precious,
ticking, and probably gold.)
In this town of telling, we grow old
in a tumble of bells, and over us all
in the continuum
time falls, snow falls, words fall.

[*The New Yorker, January 25th, 1964*]

Where Truth Lies

Maps, once made,
leave the impression of a place gone dead.

Words, once said,
anchor the swirling in the head.

Vows, once taken,
waste in the shadows of a time forsaken.

Oh understand
how the mind's landscape grows from shifting sand,

how where we are
is half on solid ground, half head-in-air,

a twilit zone
where changing flesh and changeless ghost are one,

and what is true
lies between you and the idea of you -

a friction,
restless, between the fact and the fiction

[*The New Yorker, July 1st, 1966*]

FLYING TIME

The man in the seat in front
is bald. As he reclines
his spinning pate toward me,
I look up from the map
on my knee and read into his head
the red veins that connect
St Louis with Chicago,
Phoenix with Washington.
A coastline of gray hair surrounds
his neat, skintight America,
luminous, like a mirror.
I cannot see his face
but might catch sight of my own,
might face my alien
and anxious eyes. Does he
hold an America in his head,
and is the man behind
reading the back of my head?
My hair obscures my mind.
The seat-belt sign is on.
The sky is letting us down.
What waits on the ground?
Some solid, sure America,
prepared to take us in
from the nowhere of the air,
bald, mad, lost as we are?

[*The New Yorker, August 7th, 1971*]

DAEDALUS

My son has birds in his head.

I know them now. I catch
the pitch of their calls, their shrill
cacophonies, their chitterings, their coos.
They hover behind his eyes and come to rest
on a branch, on a book, grow still,
claws curled, wings furled.
His is a bird world.

I learn the flutter of his moods,
his moments of swoop and soar.
From the ground I feel him try
the limits of the air—
sudden lift, sudden terror—
and move in time to cradle
his quivering, feathered fear.

At evening, in the tower,
I see him to sleep and see
the hooding-over of eyes,
the slow folding of wings.
I wake to his morning twitterings,
to the *croomb* of his becoming.

He chooses his selves—wren, hawk,
swallow or owl—to explore
the trees and rooftops of his heady wishing.
Tomtit, birdwit.
Am I to call him down, to give him
a grounding, teach him gravity?
Gently, gently.
Time tells us what we weigh, and soon enough
his feet will reach the ground.
Age, like a cage, will enclose him.
So the wise men said.

My son has birds in his head.

[*The New Yorker, January 1st, 1978*]

The Colour Of Herring

I read in the fishbooks that the herring
is black-backed and silver-sided,
is blue-flecked and silver-faceted,
is gray-green shot with silver,
is black and green and silver,
is blue and glass.
I find the herring in my hands
has all the silver of the evening,
all the blue of the bay,
all the green of the deep sea over the side.
The black may easily be in my mood.
The silver certainly flakes my sleeve.
But over my hands in its dying moment spills
the herring's blood
which, silver, green, black, blue aside,
runs unmistakably red.

Making Soup

Morning, making soup
in between work with words.

The two go well. I've gathered a sprawled vocabulary
of vegetables, bones, meat, herbs, a fruitful anthology

of raw beginnings. For the moment, the kitchen knife
is mightier than the pen. I split the bone

like a caveman. I rub match and matchbox together
to make fire, draw water from whatever spring

runs under Hampstead. Then, for a time, I'm lost
in the sleek elegance of the vegetables -

the trim white hocks of the leeks, in racecourse green,
the juice-tight, white transparency of the onions,

carrots red and wizened like old Scotsmen,
turnips with neat white spats, a knobbled parsnip,

parsley like miniature forests in fairy tales,
the faint tree-root whiff of thyme and bayleaf,

opacity of the onion, fat of the marrow bone.
The soup pot is a green mysterious lake.

The surface smiles and coughs. Now it is time
to return to the desk, to the steady simmer of words,

but bolstered, through the slow scrawl of the morning,
by the process of soup, that glutinous rich blending.

WEATHERING

I am old enough now for a tree
once planted, knee high, to have grown to be
twenty times me,

and to have seen babies marry, and heroes grow deaf—
but that's enough meaning-of-life.
It's living through time we ought to be connoisseurs of.

From wearing a face all this time, I am made aware
of the maps faces are, of the inside wear and tear.
I take to faces that have come far.

In my father's carved face, the bright eye
he sometimes would look out of, seeing a long way
through all the tree-rings of his history.

I am awed by how things weather: an oak mantel
in the house in Spain, fingered to a sheen,
the marks of hands leaned into the lintel,

the tokens in the drawer I sometimes touch—
a crystal lived-in on a trip, the watch
my father's wrist wore to a thin gold sandwich.

It is an equilibrium
which breasts the cresting seasons but still stays calm
and keeps warm. It deserves a good name.

Weathering. Patina, gloss, and whorl.
The trunk of the almond tree, gnarled but still fruitful.
Weathering is what I would like to do well.

[*New Republic, March 4th, 1978*]

James Bottle's Year

December finds him
outside, looking skyward.
The year gets a swearword.

His rage is never permanent.
By January he's out,
silent and plough-bent.

All white February,
he's in a fury
of wind-grief and ground-worry.

By March, he's back
scouring the ground for luck,
for rabbit-run and deer-track.

April is all sounds and smiles.
The hill is soft with animals.
His arms describe miles.

The local girls say
he's honeyed and bee-headed
at haytime in May.

In June,
he'll stay up late, he'll moon
and talk to children.

No one sees him in July.
At dawn, he'll ride away
with distance in his eye.

In August, you'd assume
yourself to be almost welcome.
He keeps open time.

But, on one September morning,
you'll see cloud-worries form.
His eyes flash storm warnings.

October is difficult.
He tries to puzzle out
If it's his or the season's fault.

In November, he keeps still
through hail and snowfall,
thinking through it all.

What's causing the odd weather?
Himself, or the capricious air?
Or the two together?

December, breathing hard,
he's back outside, hurling skyward
his same swearword.

[*The New Yorker, December 15th, 1975*]

Old (1973)

Lean, mean year, breeder of obituaries.
Funereal year, you earned a black border.
Half-masted year, we thankfully cover you over.

You claimed the long-lived ones, Casals, Picasso;
Neruda and Chile both, in one rank breath.
You gorged yourself on armies, tribes, and children.

Robbing the present to enrich the past,
you leave us as a string of cruel ciphers.
Your notes and dates are permanent in stone.

Corrosive months, counting us down in deathbells.
Gray ghoulish months of crows and cruel weather.
Meat-eating months, you trained us in despair.

Although we spite you now by seeing you out,
be confident that you will be remembered,
bitch year, burier, bearer of famous dark.

NEW (1974)

All there is of you so far
is name and number,
and a blank diary, ready for day-wear.

Imprudent to guess your progress
or clutter up your days
with hopes, oaths or wishes.

Age hands us no rule of thumb;
but so far, with clear days to come,
new year, you are welcome

[Both *Old* and *New* published as Old Year
in *The Listener, December 27th, 1973*]

THAT DYING: NOVEMBER 23, 1963

As often as not, on fair days, there is time
for words to flex their muscles, to strut like peacocks,
discovering what to say in the act of saying—
the music of meaning emerging from the sound
of the words playing.

Every now and again, however, the glass breaks,
the alarm shrills, the women hide their faces.
It is then that words jump to their feet and rush,
like white-faced stretcher-bearers,
tight-lipped, tense, to the unspeakable scene.
They grab air, water, syllables, anything handy.
There is blood. No nonsense. No adjectives. No time.

O that words could have been
a tourniquet of a kind, to keep
that exuberant life from spattering away,
instead of, as now, a dirge, a bell
tolling, a stutter, a sigh, silence.

There is nothing now for these words to do
but walk away aimlessly, mute, like mourners.

[*The New Yorker, April 25th, 1964*]

STALEMATE

Shrill interruption
of children's voices
raised in the garden.
Two of them stand
face to face,
each in one hand
weighing a stone,
each on his own
rigid ground.

You drop your stone,
then I'll drop mine.
No, you first.
Put yours down.
But if I do,
you'll throw yours.
Promise I won't.
I don't believe you.
Cross your heart?
Cross my heart.

Easy to call
the children in
before blows fall,
but not to settle

the ruffled feel
the garden has
as they both echo
the endless bicker
of lovers and statesmen,
learnt so soon.

Who began it?
Now, no matter.
The air is taut
with accusation.
Despair falls
like a cold stone
crossing the heart.
How did it start?
A children's quarrel.
What is its end?
The death of love.
The doom of all.

Black Holes

It happens on a walk. Quite suddenly
a black hole of horror opens in the road

as I recall a cruelty I did
and gasp as the hole engulfs me, the horror chokes me.

I cry out at the memory. The shame
grows hot enough to sear me.

I keep a collection of those painful moments.
Shame's a proper servant of clarity.

Sweating, I usher a surprised old woman
across the road, avoiding the black hole.

The Fall

He teeters along the crumbling top
of the garden wall and calls, "Look up,
Papa, look up! I'm flying …" till,
in a sudden foreseen spasm, I see him fall.

Terrible
when fear cries to the senses, when the whirl
of the possible drowns the real. Falling
is a fright in me. I call
and move in time to catch
his small, sweat-beaded body,
still thrilled with the air.
"I flew, Papa, I flew!"
"I know, child, I know."

[The New Yorker, June 1st, 1968]

Querida Mañana

Mañana—and an accompanying
cosmic shrug to say:
May this small incantation
keep what is still to happen
suitably far away.

In this rock-cluttered valley,
where sheep-bells tinkle time
irregularly on the ear,
and where a call will carry
across to the opposite hill,
all hangs in a continuum,
and what will happen, what befall,
seems more a matter of accident
than ever of will.

Mañana. Dear tomorrow.
The unknown in a nutshell,
invoked to give us breath,
to slough decision off,
to keep the world of Yes and No
at least a day away.

So, when the children
come trailing hopefully in

with question-marks for eyes,
looking for a word
to hang their wishing on,
mañana reassures them.
They echo it like a spell.
Tomorrow, at a distance,
will certainly be well.

[*The New Yorker, April 15th, 1967*]

VISITING LECTURER

As travelling becomes arriving,
I land, with language in my luggage,
a change of tense, to make sense of a place,
to make myself intelligible. A page
of plans turns into people, faces, voices;
and, once unpacked, my words explore
the oddness of the air,
the face the place wears and the weather
settling into staying. All the names
provide a new vocabulary, to answer
who I am, what is what, where we are.

In the lull between seeing and saying,
I wonder at the way words have
of hardening and betraying:
but sense and sound assert themselves
beyond conclusion and become
a temporary, articulated home,
a resting-place
aloof from time and space.

But only for a time. Time tells
itself through spells and sudden oracles,
and afterwards I gather
folding vocabularies

and stuff an itinerant syntax
into a silent file.
Even though words are portable,
where can they come to rest?

At best,
time dwindles down, and words
prepare to be goodbyes, and then take up
their stations in the book.
The place remains in a diary and the mind,
moving, continues undefined.

Home
is where new words are still to come.

[*The New Yorker, June 15th, 1968*]

THE ACADEMY

I do not think of the academy
in the whirl of days. It does not change. I do.
The place hangs in my past like an engraving.
I went back once to lay a wreath on it,
and met discarded selves I scarcely knew.

It has a lingering aura, leather bindings,
a smell of varnish and formaldehyde,
a certain dusty holiness in the cloisters.
We used to race our horses on the sand
away from it, manes flying, breathing hard.

Trailing to the library of an afternoon,
we saw the ivy crawling underneath
the labyrinthine bars on the window ledges.
I remember the thin librarian's look of hate
as we left book holes in her shelves, like missing teeth.

On evenings doomed by bells, we felt the sea
creep up, we heard the temperamental gulls
wheeling in clouds about the kneeworn chapel.
They keened on the knifing wind like student souls.
Yet we would dent the stones with our own footfalls.

Students still populate the place, bright starlings,
their notebooks filled with scribbled parrot-answers
to questions they unravel every evening
in lamplit pools of spreading argument.
They slash the air with theory, like fencers.

Where is the small, damp-browed professor now?
Students have pushed him out to sea in a boat

of lecture-notes. Look, he bursts into flame!
How glorious a going for one whose words
had never struck a spark on the whale-road.

And you will find retainers at their posts,
wearing their suits of age, brass buttons, flannel,
patrolling lawns they crop with careful scissors.
They still will be in silver-haired attendance
to draw lines through our entries in the annals.

It is illusion, the academy.
In truth, the ideal talking-place to die.
Only the landscape keeps a sense of growing.
The towers are floating on a shifting sea.
You did not tell the truth there, nor did I.

Think of the process—moments becoming poems
which stiffen into books in the library,
and later, lectures, books about the books,
footnotes and dates, a stone obituary.
Do you wonder that I shun the academy?

It anticipates my dying, turns to stone
too quickly for my taste. It is a language
nobody speaks, refined to ritual:
the precise writing on the blackboard wall,
the drone of requiem in the lecture hall.

I do not think much of the academy
in the drift of days. It does not change. I do.
This poem will occupy the library
but I will not. I have not done with doing.
I did not know the truth there, nor did you.

[*The New Yorker, March 21st, 1977*]

A Lesson In Handwriting

Try first this figure 2,
how, from the point of the pen,
clockwise it unwinds itself
downward to the line,
making itself a pedestal to stand on.
Watch now. Before your eyes it becomes a swan
drifting across the page, its neck so carefully
poised, its inky eye
lowered in modesty.
As you continue, soon,
between the thin blue lines,
swan after swan sails beautifully past you,
margin to margin, 2 by 2 by 2,
a handwritten swirl of swans.
Under them now unroll
the soft, curled pillows of the 6's,
the acrobatic 3's, the angular 7's,
the hourglass 8's and the neat tadpole 9's,
each passing in review
on stilts and wheels and platforms
in copybook order.

Turn the page, for now
comes the alphabet, an eccentric
parade of odd characters. Initially you may tangle

now and again in a loop or a twirl,
but patience, patience. Each in time will dawn
as faces and animals do, familiar,
laughable, crooked, quirky.
Begin with the letter S. Already
it twists away from the point like a snake or a
        watchspring,
coiled up and back to strike. SSSS, it says,
hissing and slithering off into the ferns of the F's.
Next comes a line of stately Q's floating
just off the ground, tethered by their tails,
over the folded arms of the W's
and the akimbo M's. Open-eyed, the O's
roll after them like bubbles or balloons
flown by the serious three-tongued E's.
See now how the page fills up
with all the furniture of writing—the armchair H's,
the ladders and trestles of A's and Y's and X's,
the T-shaped tables and the upholstered B's.
The pen abandons a whole scaffolding
of struts and braces, springs and balances,
on which will rest eventually
the weight of a written world, storey on storey
of words and signatures, all the long-drawn-out telling
that pens become repositories of.
These are now your care, and you may give them
whatever slant or human twist you wish,
if it should please you. But you will not alter
their scrawled authority, durable
as stone, silent, grave, oblivious
of all you make them tell.

Tomorrow, words begin.

[*The New Yorker, September 30th, 1961*]

TRANSLATOR TO POET
FOR PABLO NERUDA, 1904—1973

There are only the words left now. They lie like tombstones
or the stone Andes where the green scrub ends.
I do not have the heart to chip away
at your long lists of joy, which alternate
their iron and velvet, all the vegetation
and whalebone of your chosen stormy coast.
So much was written hope, with every line
extending life by saying, every meeting
ending in expectation of the next.
It was your slow intoning voice which counted,
bringing a living Chile into being
where poetry was bread, where books were banquets.
Now they are silent, stony on the shelf.
I cannot read them for the thunderous silence,
the grief of Chile's dying and your own,
death being the one definitive translation.

What Gets Lost | Lo Que Se Pierde

I keep translating *traduzco continuamente*
entre palabras words *que no son las mias*
into other words which are mine *de palabras a mis palabras.*
Y finalmente de quien es el texto?
Who do words belong to?
Del escritor o del traductor writer, translator
o de los idiomas or to language itself?
Traductores, somos fantasmas que viven
entre aquel mundo y el nuestro
translators are ghosts who live
in a limbo between two worlds
pero poco a poco me ocurre
que el problema no es cuestion
de lo que se pierde en traducion
the problem is not a question
of what gets lost in translation
sino but rather *lo que se pierde*
what gets lost
entre la ocurrencia—sea de amor o de agonia
between the happening of love or pain
y el hecho de que llega
a existir en palabras
and their coming into words.

Para nosotros todos, amantes, habladores
for lovers or users of words
el problema es este this is the difficulty—
lo que se pierde what gets lost
no es lo que se pierde en traducion sino
is not what gets lost in translation but more
what gets lost in language itself *lo que se pierde*
en el hecho   en la lengua,
en la palabra misma.

[*The Atlantic, July 1st, 1966*]

TAKE IT FROM HERE

Whatever it is – a day or a way of happening,
a word let fall, a ghost glimpsed in the fire,
a *déja vu*, a face, or even thinking -
from it, a poem can start,
like this one, can acquire
existence, half on paper, half in air.

A poem is the subject of itself,
but, taking this poem, this page
dappled with words, it asks
Did it happen? Will it be? Is it true?
All, all is residue.
Where any poem may go
is, somehow, somewhere,
into the air, into the listening ear.
Poems are made to disappear
into a dawning in the head.
Forget what this poem said.
Go on. Take it from here.

AND FINALLY

High Treason
by José Emilio Pacheco

I do not love my country. Its abstract splendour
is beyond my grasp.
But (although it sounds bad) I would give my life
for ten places in it, for certain people,
seaports, pinewoods, castles,
a run-down city, gray, grotesque,
various figures from its history,
mountains
(and three or four rivers).

["*Alta traición*," *TARDE O TEMPRANO (Poemas 1964–2000)*
© Herederos de José Emilio Pacheco]

Three poems by Judas Roquín

Insomnia

In that wordless limbo before sleep falls,
when ancient fears come back
to eat away the smooth facade of silence,
and trouble it – do this:
think of the word for 'thunder' in seven languages,
then seven more,
and when you arrive at *ukkonen* in Finish,
the silence which will consume you
will be, I promise you,
deeper than sleep, deeper than any dark.

Intersection

At the crossroads, I direct the word traffic
which comes at me from seventeen directions.
There are breakdowns, there are incidents, there are
accidents, the terrible crash, silence.

Only Seven To Remain Standing
(sign on a bus)

Boarding the bus, I find myself hoping
that wherever it goes, to Helsingfors or home,
across black fields, bare estuaries,
across the frozen wastes of the Sahara,
or into space, like a greenhouse on fire,
that I will be among
the seven to remain standing.

WHITHORN MANSE

I knew it as Eden,
that lost walled garden,
past the green edge
of priory and village;
and, beyond it, the house,
withdrawn, white,
one window alight.

Returning, I wonder,
idly, uneasily,
what eyes from inside
look out now, not in,
as once mine did,
and what might grant me
a right of entry?

Is it never dead, then,
that need of an Eden?

Even this evening,
estranged by age,
I ogle that light
with a child's greed,
wistfully claiming
lost prerogatives
of homecoming.

NOTES

NOTES ON THE POEMS

CALL BACK THE DAYS (EARLY POEMS)

This is the first time this grouping of poems has appeared. They must have been written roughly between the ages of seventeen and twenty two, but they already show a skilled practitioner and a reader. The title is mine (as is the order in which the poems appear). It reflects something in the poems that is unusual in AR's work – a looking backwards and a sense of turbulence in the natural world. They reflect the war in a way that is aslant; gaining resonance in their reserve in the way that Edward Thomas' poems do. 'The New Way' recalls (or is in conversation with) Thomas' work.

AR (aged seventeen) was in the Royal Navy – first on a mine-sweeper in the Irish Sea – then on what is called a Sloop in the Indian Ocean. Home port was Colombo in Ceylon/Sri Lanka. He was an able seaman, then became a lieutenant and a cipher clerk. Cipher clerks had their own office. In August of 1945, while in the South Moluccan Straits, he decoded the message: "Cease all offensive operations against the Japanese." It was repeated several times and his ship was then ordered into Singapore. It was the first Royal Navy ship into Singapore. After the war, his ship was ordered to "show the flag" in Basra. AR didn't get home until 1946.[22]

---

22   I am grateful to Leslie Clark for this information on AR's wartime service.

From then on, there is a determination not to be caught up in the shadows of the past: the direction of travel will be through time, not back in time. In 'Poem for My Father', in his first full collection, he will write, 'I choose to achieve spring, to work against winter.' Again, much later (1975), in a note to his draft of 'My Father, Dying' (in the NLS), he writes, 'I decided early/ to make my own fate, not assume the one that weighed on Scotland.'

TO LIGHTEN MY HOUSE
(NEW YORK, MORGAN AND MORGAN, 1953)

The leap from the heightened romanticism of *12 Poems* to the work of *To Lighten My House* is, as I suggested in the introduction, due to two factors: the depth of experience AR had to draw on, represented by the 'war poems' printed here, and his discovery of America. 'There is nothing like immersion in an unknown – new places, new landscapes, new preoccupations, new loves, a new language – to sharpen the edge of attention'.[23] AR never kept a diary and his essays are, by their nature, too considered to catch the immediacy of the moment. For that, we can go to the letters. The extracts which follow the Notes are from letters to his close university friend, John Main. They show a *significant* appetite for 'what's new?' that AR retained all his life.

To Lighten My House is unusual in containing extended poems and sequences: 'Designs for Three Dancers', 'Four Figures for the Sea' (part of a sequence of sea poems) and 'Directions for a Map'. Only the opening section of this last poem will be reprinted. Perhaps the learned references within the other sections of the poem (AR's degree was in classics) is what led AR to restrict its publication. AR may have come to view such references as what *The New Yorker* termed, 'incidental intelligence'. Whatever, it is

---

23   From 'Borges and Neruda' (*Inside Out*)

clear that AR will decide that the single lyric, not an extended meditation, is his favoured form. There is another notable change after this volume. AR will forego experiments in form – in the playfulness of pattern-making. In its place will be a trusting to phrasing, lineation and rhythm: the work of the ear. As his later poems show, in his subtle control of rhyme, he aimed for a diction that concealed his artistry.

Oddments, Inklings, Omens, Moments
(boston/toronto, little, brown and company, 1959)

'Poet with Sea Horse'
AR met Graves by chance in Mallorca in 1953 and remained close to him until, in 1961, he 'ran off' with Margot Callas, one of Graves' muses. In his essay, 'Remembering Robert Graves',[24] AR acknowledges Graves' importance to him as a poet, prose-writer and translator. It was the model of Graves that persuaded AR to live by writing. Together, they wrote *Quoz – a Correspondence 1955-56*, an exchange of letters between thirty two year old AR and sixty year old Graves. In one of the early letters, AR offers a definition of 'Quoz' as, 'apparently a word which, given various intonations, served the general purpose of disintegrating thoroughly any remarks made to one, a kind of verbal clothing for a rude sound.' This leads to a lengthy disquisition on the part of Graves. The ms is in the NLS, unpublished.

'Who Am I?'
The poem brings to mind these lines from 'Portrait of a Lady' by T. S. Eliot:
  'I feel like one who smiles, and turning shall remark
  Suddenly his expression in a glass.'
AR read widely and conversed with what he read.

---

24   In *Outside In* (Edinburgh, Polygon, 2008)

'In Memory of My Uncle Timothy'

This makes a companion piece to the previously unpublished, 'Aunt Elsie' placed in Poems from *Weathering*. AR didn't write many poems about family; these and poems about his father, grandfather and son.

'The Tale The Hermit Told'

AR shared the fruitful inheritance of Scotland's oral literature with W. S. Graham, one of AR's favourite poets; one who had also felt compelled to leave Scotland and one also, at one point, influenced by Dylan Thomas. On the other hand, 'A Homecoming' shows that AR's narrative imagination could also draw on 'the tale' of Ulysses.

Poems from PASSWORDS: Places, Poems, Preoccupations (boston/toronto, little, brown and company, 1963)

'A Lesson in Music'

This poem was in fact published in *Passwords* with the title, 'To A Child at the Piano'. It is republished in *Weathering* with the title, 'A Lesson in Music', presumably to allow its wider resonances. As a widely anthologised poem, it appears here with its more common name.

'Me To You'

This poem is unusual in that it is the only one of AR's works that will be published in an extended version, in *Weathering*. Both versions are included in this collected to allow the reader to see the changes AR's ear has made to the longer one and to restore the second part, which I imagine length precluded from *Passports*.

'The O Filler'

The 'The O Filler' was based on a real encounter. In his introduction to *When Now Is Not Now* (Poetry Trust, 2006), AR writes,

'My constant preoccupations have been with languages, with human oddness and eccentricity, with villages and the agrarian round, and with what geographers call "land-life relations".''The O Filler' certainly has a place among these!

Poems from WEATHERING
(EDINBURGH, CANONGATE PUBLISHING, 1978)

Weathering is selected from AR's poetry and translations. The new poems appear here in the order they do in *Weathering*. AR claimed, rather mischievously and misleadingly, that, 'the poems are not arranged in any particular order, chronological or otherwise'. AR's friend and agent, Thomas Colchie, commented to me in an email (15/3/16) that AR 'was very thematic minded and saw each book as a creative entity of a certain time and place in his crafting. But he never particularly ruled out works that were left behind in a previous typesetting and looked back on each artefact of his development with continuing appreciation and affection. That is to say, he never ceased to redefine his work, but likewise never intellectually discarded the many framings of his writing. Each volume served its purpose as the best take on himself at the particular time of its inception.'

The contents list can be found here, the new poems underlined.[25] I have added to the new poems five poems previously unpublished or uncollected (asterisked on *Barefoot's* contents page), placing them where they sit best.

'The Manse'
This is the manse in Selkirk. In 'Hauntings', AR describes how he had found only 'a surviving sliver of the garden wall, a thin, teetering pillar of stone …What haunts me most of all, however, is that the house has not gone, nor have our memories been wiped clean of it. All I would have to do is find the thread ends and slowly reel it all in, from dark to light …'

'My Father, Dying'.
The last thought in 'Poem for My Father', the second poem in *To Lighten Up My House*, is the poet reaching, 'with his [father's] hands to bless again the bare potential earth'. Now, in this anticipated

---

elegy, he reflects on his relationship with this 'dear old man'. For this poem, AR made extensive preparatory notes in prose, which he termed, 'working papers'. In one of these he noted, 'it is only curiosity that is keeping [my father] alive.' There are numerous drafts of the poem, and for the title poem of the collection too, in the large ledgers AR favoured (Bushey Sketch Books for Pen or Pencil with perforated leaves, 20x14 inches) as he worked at what he wanted to say until the poem, through technique and feeling, fitted the human voice. AR told me once that the sound of the human voice moved him far more than music. Writing of Borges, in his essay 'Neruda and Borges' (*Outside In*), he says, 'In many conversations with Borges, from the formal to the fanciful, I realised sharply that to him I only existed as a voice. That may have led to my deep conviction that voice is perhaps the most essential and lasting incarnation of any existence.' You can hear AR's own 'incarnation' in recordings made for The Poetry Archive.

'Scotland'

This poem's original title was 'St Andrews'. AR became so tired of reading it, while believing it represented a Scotland that no longer existed, that, in 2007, at StAnza, St Andrews' poetry festival, he announced his final reading of it and thereafter set the poem alight. The act was, in many ways, a fitting conclusion to AR's fractious but persistent relationship with Scotland. Among his papers at the NLS, there is a copy of a boldly and, judging by the handwriting, hastily conceived, but teasing, project:

> We, the undersigned, MURIEL SPARK, and ALASTAIR REID do hereby agree to commit six weeks of their lives, beginning on an agreed date in December 1965, to writing, IN CONJUNCTION, a piece of writing involving their CONJOINT experiences and thereabouts, in SCOTLAND, an unconquered autonomous realm within the BRITISH ISLANDS. The undersigned TWAIN do hereby agree to devote their entire energies, physical, spir-

itual and mental, to the achievement of that same artefact, within the stated period to the benefit of humanity, and to the enlightenment of the HUMAN RACE, with appropriate gratitude to THE NEW YORKER MAGAZINE. Signed: this day Sunday 23rd May 1965:

They sign themselves, 'scriveners'.

'Making Soup'.
This is an unpublished poem. AR once commented that some poems are like recipes that get passed from hand to hand. 'Making Soup' - which AR frequently did - a recipe about writing, deserves to be more widely distributed.

'Old and New'
These two were published as a greeting to the New Year in 1974. 'Old' appears in *Weathering* as '1973'. Here they are restored together.

'That Dying'
I have retained AR's contrary chronological inversion here, ie 1973 preceding 1963.

A note on the poem, 'That Dying' (AR)[26]

> Early in 1964, some two months after the assassination of President Kennedy, an American publisher wrote to a number of poets in Britain and the United States to enquire whether any of them had written, or contemplated writing, a poem on the tragic event of the assassination. Some poems had indeed appeared immediately after the event, and the publishers drew attention to the fact that a large memorial volume of verse had been published three months after the assassination of Abraham Lincoln.

---

26 *Of Poetry and Power: Poems Occasioned by the Presidency and by the Death of John F. Kennedy*, edited by Erwin A. Glikes and Paul Schwaber (Basic Books, Inc, New York, 1964).

I received the letter in Buenos Aires, and my first reaction was one of faint horror at the idea. I had felt the loss keenly but had not written about it; it would be improbable now, I thought, to conjure up a poem in retrospect. I had found the assassination so appalling as to feel that there was nothing whatsoever to say about it; to me, it had been truly inconceivable, like bad fiction. As I travelled north, I thought a few times about the matter and wondered exactly what poets do in the face of public tragedy. Then it dawned on me that the fact of not being able to utter anything might be the substance of a poem. One evening (I was in Mexico City) I was thinking again about this when I suddenly saw words themselves as spectators, whereas they are usually actors in a poem. I could see the words themselves as witnesses to the tragedy, and the poem began to occur, a poem about the behaviour of words. I wrote it in Mexico, and sent it to the editors. Later on, I reworked it a little and sent it to *The New Yorker*, where it was published. *The New Yorker* version and the version published in the book, POETRY AND POWER, differ here and there, and I have never been able to decide between them. In the worksheet of the poem, however, most of the variations are already present.

As a footnote, AR once told me that he had written the preface to *Weathering* to deflect expectation from questions about when the next book was coming. In the same way, the back cover of *Oddments . . .* states, 'At present he is completing a novel.' He told me that was a fiction, yet in one of his letters to John Main (from Bustins Island, Maine on 12 July, 1950), he writes, 'I have begun a novel which is a frightful thing to do, because it tears things out of the middle of you, forces you to lay things down.' In the archive at the NLS, I found the first pages of a novel, *ICSYLF*. It has an unreliable translator as narrator.

AND FINALLY –

'High Treason'

Barefoot is concerned with AR's own poetry. He himself always kept his translated work separate, within its own volumes or clearly demarcated within the same volume, as in *Weathering* and *Inside Out*. There were no 'imitations', or poems fashionably 'after', interleaved with his own. He translated, at the least, several examples of a poet's work; in Neruda's and Borges' cases, considerably more and always the aim was to render poems that he felt could 'stand on their own as English poems'. And it is worth emphasising that the translations were deep, empathetic explorations. Mike Gonzalez, who knew AR well and the works he translated, commented in his obituary: 'His translations were much more than versions or homages; he was a travelling companion and an interlocutor to the monstrous presences he chose or rather who chose him, not to interpret their poems but to rediscover them and give them new life in another language. He built not only collaborations, but friendships with Borges, Neruda and the finest Latin American poets.'[27]

As 'What Gets Lost' states, 'translators are ghosts who live/ in a limbo between two worlds', a limbo in which there could be transferences and identifications between poet and translator. The inclusion of 'High Treason' by Mexican poet, José Emilio Pacheco, serves as the sole, but necessary, representative here of the permeability of sensibility to which translation can lead. In introducing the poem in his essay, 'Digging Up Scotland', AR writes that he came across the poem in a book of Pacheco's he was translating and that it 'so coincided with a poem I myself might have written that while I was translating it I felt I was writing the original.'

---

27 *Variaciones Borges* (Pittsburgh University, 2014)

Three poems by Judas Roquín
The pithy and often surreal poems of the Costa Rican poet, Judas Roquín, deserve acknowledgement as an interesting adjunct to AR's work. Roquín also crops up in prose pieces AR has written. In one of these, we learn that Roquín himself meets AR in the same Mexico City apartment in which he, Roquín, had met Max Aub in 1964. AR writes that 'we had crossed each other's path for years.' In another piece, 'Latin American Fictions', which AR wrote while a fellow at the Woodrow Wilson International Center for Scholars (1986-87), AR quotes, 'from [his] translation of a passage in the Journals of Judas Roquín, the Costa Rican writer, since it coincides with my own experience in the Dominican Republic.'

'Judas Roquín' is what happens when a poet and translator goes rogue. The invented writer shows AR's love of play, of creating *ficciones*. It was only when interest in Roquín grew too intense that AR dissolved his ghost.

'Whithorn Manse'
This is the last poem I'm aware of AR having written. It was published as a postcard on Scotland's National Poetry Day in 1999 and in *Inside Out* (2008). The poem is a reworking of 'Childhood Landscape' from *Oddments*... The poem has passed through time, so that the phrase 'estranged from age' gains fresh emotional impetus. The naming of the title too is significant, recalling T. S. Eliot's lines from 'Little Gidding':

> ...the end of all our exploring
> Will be to arrive where we started
> And know the place for the first time.

The disenchantment of *Weathering's* preface, signalling his long silence, was not the first expression of AR's reservations about poetry as a public act. In a letter to John Main, in 1950, he comments, 'I see poetry as an art-form that is dying. The poet is looking for symbols for his world: and since these become more and more difficult to find, poetry becomes more and more private.' In the NLS, I come across a torn scrap of paper on which a draft of 'St. Andrews' is written. On its reverse, I read:

> Poems are stages in the life of a poet. But poets' lives are usually uneven lives. The durable poets are those with a ranging curiosity and a ranging technique, so that the exercise of writing a poem can keep them going when the impulse is not strong. Most poets have hectic periods of a few years when everything is in tune – then fallow periods where they either imitate themselves or write only occasional poems. Myself [.,]

I peer for a long time, but cannot make out whether the ink mark is a comma or a slurred, hesitant full-stop. It is an appropriate ambiguity on which to end. But, whatever its intent, AR never gave up his love of and commitment to poetry itself. One of his final projects – and one that brought him great pleasure – was working with his friend, the Mexican poet Pura López Colomé. They faced each other with a sheaf of favourite poems in English and Spanish and, through conversation, arrived at translations which they recorded in a three CD set: *Entre Voces: Resonancia: Poésia en Dos Lenguas.* It is a delight.

FROM *UNPUBLISHED LETTERS* FROM ALASTAIR REID TO JOHN MAIN, 1949-1951.

The *Scotsman* obituary of John Main (1920-1988) lists him as 'sailor, man of the theatre, diplomat, academic'. He was, by all accounts, something of a celebrity as a student at St. Andrews. In his letters, AR shared with him his experiences and aspirations, as they had both shared a sense of playfulness. The obituary tells us that, 'Irritated by earnest music lovers who followed concerts in the Younger Hall with the score in hand, he and his friend, the poet Alastair Reid, would take along gramophone records which they would pretend to follow by scraping a finger nail along the grooves.'

Cedar Falls, Iowa, 9.9.49
This America is something.

New York has all the excitement of tall buildings and a kind of magical atmosphere. I met hundreds of delightful people, wrote some things and generally lived in all senses, stimulated, intrigued, fascinated, interested and sharpened …Washington …has a firm white pattern, but had all the aloofness and insouciance of a monument. I just can't gaze at things that are meant to be gazed at.

Cedar Falls is a little slow, tree-lined wooden Mid-west town with quiet streets and a drowsy gentle air …The wheels in my head turn as busily here, sometimes in new revolutions.

John, I think next year I'll go to Yale to begin work on a PhD.

9.10.49
I've discovered lots of things. Mainly that I like lecturing. The little Iowans have a naivety that is charming. Things unfold in their faces …The staff get better and better …Nothing is accepted. Everything is challenged, beaten out, substantiated …And this campus is beautiful. The leaves are red and yellow, wild with autumn and sun and blue sky sets them off every day. There are trees as tall as God, and great hoarse bells that whisper in at the windows as I sit and write.

I have never felt so free and uncomplicated I think …I feel that at last I don't belong to anything but the thing inside me.

It is Sunday night, my brooding night.

8.11.49

The more I have to do with academic institutions, the less I think I will remain in them. Anything will do – farm, boats, gardens are probably best – but if there is the academic atmosphere, it keeps turning in on itself more and more – the snake eating its own tail, until finally <u>there is no life left</u>, and the question comes, what <u>is</u> this life we are talking about? …I have no idea how long I'll stay. I think perhaps no more than two years. I'm beginning to be ready to write bigger things now. Someday I'll start to write them.

Don't go and get into the civil service or anything. And if you have any project that you think might interest me, tell me, and I'll be there like a shot. I think Iscia (sic) is the answer.

19.12.49

I never regretted it going down and grubbing in the dust, a level removed from anything actual and sensuous and real. I appreciated it, for it made me so glad of the light.

I plan to stay another year, then I'll probably come home and make a noise, or try to.

15.1.50

In September I'm coming to New York City to live for the year, doing nothing but writing, painting and things. This because New York is the most absorbing, stimulating, exciting place I have ever struck, <u>humanly</u> speaking.

I have a great desire to be poor again, and a great desire to leave all the ordinary things for other people to do.

??.2.50

I'm getting obsessed, John, with the idea of getting one's hands in. <u>Of doing</u>. I'm pretty certain that in May I'll be leaving the academic life not just for a year but for a long long time. It involves compromise and I'm beginning to hate compromise so much, for I see a great deal of it all round me.

I think that, at the end of things, it's going to be an Ischia. Not because of anything more than the <u>reality</u> of it, for it would be a complete life. It would entail being an Ischian: it would have to.

1.2.50
I know this — that there is an essential connection between my life and my poetry. If I am constipated or dumb, if I stutter or gush, I know the pattern of my life is wrong. This relationship with the world is a living, changing thing, and I know that the conceptual world we create in philosophy is false completely — nothing exists like it. Experience will <u>not</u> be forced into such a pattern, if we are true to it.

There is no us, nor any world — only the relationship, the world-in-us ...It doesn't matter not writing. The <u>living</u> matters.

4.9.50
John, I've been writing <u>poetry</u> now. All the past stuff is forgotten. Now I know what it's all about. I was at an incredible poets' gathering in Harvard where I spent a lot of time with Stephen Spender and Pierre Emmanuel and got seized with a great passion for poetry. So I came back to New York and have been writing like a wild man ever since. It's great, like being drunk all the time. But I'm going to have to take a job. I have $1000 and I must have some for the new beginning next year. I can be an assistant in a tropical fish store in the next block, but I don't know.

Two things I am full of. One, a sense of the unique nature of the contemporary world, and how important it is to speak in its terms, not to drive home inconsequential meaningless old values. Two, a great passion that comes out of the earth, a passion for simplicity, for sun, for not caring much, for the tremendous full sensuous experience of being alive in one moment of time. The realisation is a business of the blood: it contains its own eternity. These and a great delight in words are all I want: and they have within them infinite poems.

29.4.51

Thank God I can leave America for a bit: it's really a desperate place. There are so many things that can make one unhappy, so many physical sights and experiences which one cannot avoid and which inevitably grow into symbols …Yes I am coming back next year: I want to be in this college another year, for I have never found a community to which I felt more like giving myself. And I learn, in the best, human way. My literary luck is changing. I sold poems to *The New Yorker* which is as high as one can go, and *Harpers* are going to bring out a book in which I am collaborating. I am still poor, but I have a possible devotion here which is everything.

…you are terribly right …The mediocre <u>will not do</u>. All the work has to be better than we are, than we know how. It can't be adjusted with an easy feeling. We have to know <u>what we feel</u> and we have to make the poems a discovery in that sense.

NOTE: The line in one letter (9.9.49), 'I just can't gaze at things that are meant to be gazed at,' expresses eloquently what Andrew O'Hagan referred to as AR's enduring 'Scots accent of the mind'.

INDEX